P9-DZA-433

# AfterCulture

# AfterCulture

## Detroit and the Humiliation of History

Jerry Herron

Wayne State University Press Detroit

99 98 97 96 95 94 93 5 4 3 2 1

Herron, Jerry, 1949–
AfterCulture : Detroit and the humiliation of history / Jerry Herron.
p. cm.
Includes bibliographical references.
ISBN 0-8143-2070-8 (alk. paper)
1. Detroit (Mich.)—Popular culture. 2. Detroit (Mich.)—Social conditions. I. Title.
F574.D45H47 1993
977.4'34—dc20 93-10873

Designer: Mary Primeau

Cover photo: The Heidelburg Project of Tyree Guyton; his wife, Karen; and Grandpa Sam MacKay. Courtesy, The Detroit Institute of Arts. Dirk Bakker, photographer.

Some sections, or parts of sections, of this book first appeared previously, in other publications, sometimes in earlier versions.

Introduction: "Niki's Window: Detroit and the Humiliation of History," *The Georgia Review*, 47.2 (Summer 1993).

Violence: "Post-Modernism Ground Zero, or Going to the Movies at the Grand Circus Park, *Social Text*, 18 (Winter 1987): 61–77.

Renewal: "Popular Culture/Popular Violence: Postmodernism and the Malling of Semiotics," *Mimesis, Semiosis, and Power.* Edited by Ronald Bogue. John Benjamins Publishing Company, Amsterdam/Philadelphia, 1991: 185–206.

The author wishes gratefully to acknowledge permission to quote from the following poems.

"It's Not Me Shouting at No One" is reprinted from *Shouting at No One*, by Lawrence Joseph, by permission of the University of Pittsburgh Press. © 1983 by Lawrence Joseph.

"#107 'monk's dream' for tyree & karen guyton & sam mackey" by John Sinclair is quoted form *thelonious: a book of monk.* © 1989, 1993 John Sinclair. All rights reserved. Reprinted with permission of the author.

Excerpts from "Direct Address" by Barrett Watten reprinted from *Conduit*, © Barrett Watten 1988.

"The Passionate Shopping Mall," by Charles Baxter, from *Imaginary Paintings and Other Poems.* Copyright 1989 by Charles Baxter, published by British American Publishing, 19 British American Blvd., Latham, NY 12110.

**for Carol**

# Contents

# Preface

This is a book about Detroit; it is also, unavoidably, a book about representation because Detroit is the most representative city in America. Detroit used to stand for success, and now it stands for failure. In that sense, the city is not just a physical location; it is also a project, a projection of imaginary fears and desires. This is the place where bad times get sent to make them belong to somebody else; thus, it seems easy to agree about Detroit because the city embodies everything the rest of the country wants to get over. But the same things that make Detroit immediately, if disagreeably, representative also make it very hard to know because the "truth" about the place comes in prearranged form, often with little relevance to actual fact or feeling.

The history of Detroit, which is my subject, is also a history of humiliations; it is a history as humiliation. What I mean by this is summed up in the famous dictum attributed to Henry Ford, who played a large part in making Detroit what it is. Ford sued the *Chicago Tribune* for libel in 1919 because an editorial had accused him of being "ignorant." During the fourteen-week trial that followed (at the end of which he would be awarded six cents in damages), Ford supposedly delivered his celebrated dismissal: "History is bunk." He may or may not have uttered the famous words; nevertheless, making bunk out of history was surely what "Fordism" was all about, and it's what the town that became synonymous with Ford's inventions came to be about: the creation of a material plenitude so vast that people would quit worrying about the past, and history would cease to matter. Detroit's humiliation of history seemed an exhilarating idea, so long as the good times lasted, but when they ran out, it left both the city and the people in it painfully undefended and up for grabs.

Each essay that follows I intend as just that, literally —an attempt to understand the production of middle-class culture by essaying to figure out what has happened in Detroit. I am concerned with the middle class not only because most Americans (90 percent according to one recent survey) think of themselves that way but also because the institutions people generally associate with cities—museums, restaurants, movie theaters, department stores—originate in the need of the middle class to locate and reproduce itself socially. Not the least source of interest for me personally is that my own life has been informed by those same institutions. My father, who started out a working man, entrusted my future to an institutional care that would translate me, ultimately, into a college professor, whose job brought him unexpectedly—if happily—to Detroit.

I have not tried to write an exclusively academic book, although there are academic arguments throughout. Instead, I'd like to think of my project as a book of visits, some of which are to theoretical or technical sites, but the majority of which are visits to the city. I have concluded, finally, that it is not possible to write about "the city" as if that were a fixed and uniform subject. It's more accurate to think of my subject as a figure comprised of overlapping, often contradictory "moments." One person's urban renewal becomes another person's eviction, to cite a familiar example, so that the figure never resolves itself into a settled meaning. My essays don't attempt to record either the whole of urban history or even the whole history of Detroit. Although I've tried to be accurate, I have been less concerned with the facts, strictly speaking, than with the means people have developed for remembering and recording and acting on the inescapable, if elusive, fact of the past. Frequently, my "visits" return to the same site, but not, I hope, to the same ideas; I have tried to create a figure in my text that reproduces the overlaid moments I believe define the city. The essays don't necessarily have to be read in the order I have chosen, although it's probably best to read the first two before going on to the others because they develop concepts that inform the rest of the pieces.

My project would not have been possible without the support of a number of generous individuals and institutions. I wish to thank all the friends who have read and commented on parts of my manuscript, and who have been willing to talk about Detroit with me. In particular I am grateful to Charlie Baxter, who was one of the first to read my work and speak kindly, and critically, about it. From Ronald Bogue, I continue always to learn. To Arthur Marotti, a colleague of ten years' standing, I am profoundly grateful. I shall never forget the many acts of kindness and the unstinting support he has shown me and my work.

I wish to thank Arthur Evans, Director of the Wayne State University Press, who is as fine and understanding a publisher as any author could wish for. I owe a debt as well to Gerald Coyle, who is a first-rate dentist and a faultless bibliographer.

For their generous support of my research, I wish to thank the William Dean Howells Memorial. And for support not only of this project, but of my career generally, I owe much to my department and to Wayne State University, and to the chair of my department, Les Brill, whom I count a good friend.

Finally, and most of all, I find myself, happily, in the debt of Carol Guither, as patient and generous a collaborator as ever there was.

# Introduction

## The Sign in Niki's Window

*"We as a nation seem to be self-destructing—environmentally, economically and culturally. Detroit is just doing it more quickly and more willfully."*

—Marvin Krueger in a letter to the *New York Times*

### I

Who could have guessed the sign in Niki's window? Nobody, I expect, and that's both the wonder of it, and also the shame. Niki's sign tells the truth, the whole truth. It faithfully represents what it stands for, which is all the things that have happened to history in Detroit, the most historically representative city in America: the one place that everybody else can agree on by agreeing they no longer want any part of it. Not when they think about what has gone on, and gone wrong, here: riots and white flight, plant closings and industrial collapse, murders and carjackings, assaults, arson, and drug wars—all the kinds of trouble that people who've left the city were hoping to leave behind. And unlike Los Angeles, say, or Washington, D.C., the troubles here are not relieved by the operatic distractions of a Hollywood or a national government.

Eloquence notwithstanding, Niki's sign goes largely unnoticed. Maybe that's because no one, individually, is responsible for creating this remarkable device; unlike most historical texts, there's no author to claim credit for its prodigal intelligence. Or maybe the sign gets ignored because it is so clearly a reminder of unwanted things. Or maybe it's just that the moment for this sign has not yet come. Niki's sign records a city that nobody has figured out how to need, or even tolerate, for that matter: a city that appears after the culture of middle-class expectations that once sustained America gives way and falls apart.

Detroit—more than any other spot in this country—has been so thoroughly humiliated by history, so emptied of the content, both material and human, that used to make this place *mean*, that it becomes questionable whether the city still exists at all in any practical sense. "Neighborhoods collapsed," the mayor blustered at a TV interviewer when pressed about the problems that plague Detroit, "because half the goddam population left" ("Detroit's Agony"). Inevitably, then, a sign that stands in for Detroit—a place where fewer than half the more than two million former residents still choose to live—is going to be problematic because recognition carries a considerable price. Everyone who lives here has become familiar with the observation (usually delivered by visitors, in a state of mild surprise): "Detroit looks just like a city!" It's easy to get defensive when people say things like that. At the same time, it's clear what they mean by their offending comparison. History, like the middle class who have usually imagined themselves its protagonists (at least for the last hundred years), has generally written off places like Detroit, so that it comes as a shock to visitors when they find something here, especially something downtown, and still in business, that they recognize as belonging to their native culture. It's like discovering a family photo at some stranger's yard sale. What a surprise: Isn't that us? Detroit looks just like a city!

The recognition, however, is not entirely happy, any more than the discovery of the photo would be: it invites an inquiry into provenance perhaps better left unpursued; it raises the suspicion that if Detroit really *were* a city—like other cities—then the things that have happened in it, and to it, might happen anywhere. And given what has gone on here, especially in terms of media coverage, the wish to have Detroit *not* be representative is powerful; this accounts for the tentative, and perhaps cautionary, observation that the place only *looks* like a city. Despite appearances, it really isn't one, at least not any longer. Detroit has to be deprived of its reality so that everybody else can feel better about theirs. "Our first story is not a story about a city," as Diane Sawyer assured America when *PrimeTime Live* came to cover Detroit: "It's a story about some Americans who may be sending a kind of warning to the rest of us. . . . Detroit, once a symbol of U.S. competitive vitality, and some say still a symbol: a symbol of the future, the first urban domino to fall" ("Detroit's Agony"). But as long as that domino remains far enough removed from the others, its falling down won't start a chain reaction, and the warning will amount to no more than that: a cautionary tale of things that only *might* happen. And it's just there, in the standing for things that needn't happen anywhere but here, that Detroit becomes essential to contemporary, American myth making.

It's as if the country needs a Detroit to go uniquely wrong in order to make clearer and simpler—by comparison—the otherwise baffling work of going right. This is the site, or the symbol, that makes consensus once more seem possible for Americans, whom differences of all kinds have driven apart. Outside of war, or some sort of national emergency, it's hard to imagine anything—especially anything domestic and urban—that people could agree on and get behind, except, perhaps, for the wish to keep "Detroit" from happening to the place where they live. The worst, in whatever form, can be un-threateningly (even titillatingly) contemplated here because, as Diane Sawyer suggested, Detroit isn't a city like other cities any more; its "story" doesn't script a necessary outcome for anybody else. At least not yet. The people of Detroit may be "sending a kind of warning," as Sawyer put it, but, more important, we're also providing an excuse. Do whatever you have to do; that's the admonition spoken in our behalf, because if you don't, you might end up like we did: black and violent, sick, abandoned, poor;

and also deprived of the history that would turn such time-serving advice into more complicated questions of cause and effect. This may be why the witness of Niki's incorruptible sign remains problematic and not entirely welcome.

## II

There's nothing mysterious about the sign—at any rate not on the surface. It's red and white letters painted on a pane of plate glass in the window of Niki's Taverna, which is an inexpensive restaurant in a part of the old business district referred to locally as "Greektown." The sign names the place as belonging to Niki: N-I-K-I-'-S. But that's where the simplicity ends. First, there is no Niki to stand behind the sign. *Niki* is the name invented by a Greek dishwasher and school dropout named Dennis Kefallinos, who immigrated to America at age fourteen, worked hard, saved his money, and now—some twenty years later—has come to own a restaurant, several parcels of real estate, and a food distribution company.

Thanks to Niki's success, Kefallinos no longer has to wash dishes. He wears suits now, and the dishwashers work for him. His photograph accompanies an article in the *Detroit News*, "Horatio Algers Without Diplomas." Niki lounges pridefully—a handsome, smiling man in his thirties—leaning against the front of his restaurant, right next to the sign. "To make it happen in this country is easier now than 30 years ago," he told the interviewer (Ingersoll B1). "Making it happen"—that's what Niki is good at, which is how he got his picture in the paper and how he qualifies as one of Detroit's "Horatio Algers Without Diplomas." The reporter has confused Alger—a philanthropic Harvard graduate—with his self-made characters, but no matter. In a way, conflation is precisely the point and the reason to congratulate the immigrant Kefallinos on his becoming Niki. Niki mocks our natives' disbelief in "Horatio Alger" clichés with the visible fact of his improvised success: "There's no such thing as, 'I can't make it happen.' I don't buy that" (B1). And why should he?

Niki's story of opportune self-creation is no less true of Greektown itself. Like the stylized waiter's portrait he uses as a logo—a kind of ethnic happy face—this historic "town" is largely make-believe. Greektown is actually just one block of Monroe Street and a block or two of a cross street, Beaubien, where Niki set up his business. This part of the city was first settled in the eighteenth century by French farmers (Antoine Beaubien, whose property line became the street in front of Niki's, being one of them); the French were followed a hundred years later by German immigrants, who arrived in great numbers after the failed revolution of 1848. The Germans were probably feeling down on their luck, and seem not to have wanted to memorialize their arrival by inventing a "Germantown" to live in. Nor were they interested in finery; the buildings they put up are architecturally undistinguished and utilitarian. Civic pride demanded something grander, something perpetually more up-to-date, to stand for the city. Consequently, this part of Detroit mostly got left alone, which is why there's enough of it still standing to be converted by entrepreneurs who want to help their neighbors rediscover the romance of the urban past. It would take quite a few years to arrive at that point, however, when the past would feel like something to capitalize, rather than conceal. And by then, the depopulation of Detroit would have so altered its demographic character (with more than 70 percent of the residents now being black and nearly a third of them living in poverty) that certain realities could best be dealt with through proxies, like the invented Niki, whose simulacral Greek waiter offers a blandly acceptable stand-in for otherwise threatening differences—of race and class—that history has left painfully unresolved.

Goings-on are unabashedly touristic in Niki's home town, where practically nobody, including Greeks, still lives. What's left of the old neighborhood has mostly been pushed aside by conversion, like the few remaining tables in the Macedonia Cafe. Video arcade games—Street Fighter II and Super Street Fighter II—have taken over the space where Greek men used to sit, playing cards, smoking cigarettes, and drinking sweet coffee out of tiny cups. Now visitors—generally white, suburban, and middle-class—come here, to the inner city, as if looking for something valuable their parents or grandparents forgot in the rush to get up and out and on to a better life. Greektown is not so much a place, then, as it is a way of reinventing one of the oldest and now most profitably "restored" parts of Detroit. No city is immune to this kind of entrepreneurial ersatz, even ones where residents pride themselves on being *genuinely* historical: Boston, New York, San Francisco, Baltimore, Philadelphia. They've all got neighborhoods like Greektown, where tourists "return" to an urban theme park to buy souvenirs of a time—usually ethnic, crowded, and working-class—that the people caught in it couldn't wait to escape. Only when looked at from outside does history seem so appealing. And similarly, it's mostly from outside that the loss of the past, which usually means the dissolving of bonds that kept somebody else in place, appears so dreadful and dislocating. As to that, plenty of unconverted memories are still being lived out in this part of town: memories of being left behind by a future that never arrived. But these find no part in the general festivities, where such a problematic witness would be interpreted as inappropriate and offensive, like the stink of the homeless man when he shelters in a public space: the sort of thing that successful conversions—like private security firms—are meant to keep outside.

## III

Greektown is where people always take out-of-town visitors, or where they go themselves, especially on summer evenings, if the weather is nice. Here, for the space of one block, Detroit puts on a recognizable, urban scene. Monroe Street is narrow, barely two lanes wide; pedestrians jay-walk leisurely among the slow-moving cars. Buildings are as old as any in the city and low, two or three stories, made of weathered red brick, with no space between. All the storefronts are filled, most with Greek restaurants and bakeries and markets, one after the other: Simeon Bakery, the Athens Bar, the Golden Fleece, the Athens Bakery, the Laikon Cafe, the Olympia, the Grecian Gardens, Pegasus Restaurant, the Hellas (which claims to be the original Greek restaurant on Monroe Street), the New Parthenon, Astoria Pastry, Aegean Ice Cream, and so on, down to the end of the block and the Romanesque towers of St. Mary's Catholic Church, the single unconverted site on the street and the only one, consequently, that requires the explanation of an historic marker.

By dinnertime, lines form out on the sidewalk, with people waiting to get into restaurants to eat, especially at the Laikon and the Hellas with its wrap-around windows. Rollerbladers cruise by on Monroe; vendors sell roses "for the lady." There's even a sketch artist who will do your portrait, and a guy in improvised Elizabethan costume who will produce a sonnet to suit the occasion. Couples stroll along, eating ice cream cones, holding hands. Conventioneers with plastic badges—"Hi! I'm Bob"—travel in packs, talking loud, after having had too much to drink: this isn't their town so it doesn't matter. They're the ones most likely to stop and stare through the window at Lindos to watch the bellydancer perform on stage. But generally the crowd is well behaved, and largely white, except for the teenagers. The average visitor to Greektown, according to a recent consumer survey, is thirty-four years old, with an income of more than $40,000, and resides in suburban Oakland County, eight miles north, where at one point there is the highest concentration of millionaires per square foot in America (Markiewicz 1992: F3). When it gets dark, twinkle lights come on in the small locust trees planted along the curb. Here, for a few hours each evening, Detroit tries to look just like a city.

Which leads to a question: If Greektown is so obviously contrived, then why does it sell? Maybe it's because the thirtysomething Americans of the baby boom are also the first fully suburbanized generation in our history. Their expectations—if not their actual lives—were sited in the green world that lay beyond the town, where the old, urban agenda of delayed gratification gave way to an Edenic plenitude that granted everyone the same sort of house, and the same sort of life, and more or less at the same time. And what was most important, that's the way people would naturally want it. Or so we allowed ourselves to believe. That postwar dream never really came true, but the moment when it seemed as if it might is the one the majority of midlife Americans grew up inside of, like the thirty-four-year-old householder from Oakland County whose visits keep Greektown in business. Our suburban utopia sited itself just at the vanishing point of history and described a state of social grace beyond which further change would not be required. There would be progress, sure, but it would be the progress of products, as Ronald Reagan used to promise on the General Electric Theater: a progress defined by the extension of markets, by the happy acceptance of built-in obsolescence, by the elaboration of sales and distribution networks; an all-white progress vouchsafed in the evangel of Ozzie and Ward and Donna Reed.

The nostalgic pull of their myth is not only powerful but also debilitating because the culture of plentiful sameness has ended up being subject to forces not comprehended by its own bland images. Syndication (and cable TV) render this very-Brady memory unavoidable, and perhaps beguiling; but unavoidable too is the realization that this nostalgic utopia is daily humiliated by the spectacle of a future that never happened. The present, in other words, has turned out to be more like the city—and like its old story of opposition and strife—than the timeless, green world beyond it, which means that the myths of the past lead not to security, but to a "fear of falling," as Barbara Ehrenreich has referred to the middle-class dread of a mobility that appears—in relation to the past—to be only downward. As a result, urban culture reemerges, as both a threat and also as a source of intelligence, regardless of how welcome or well comprehended this intelligence may be. Because cities have always stood for something larger than individual existence, they again become significant when being an individual seems to mean less, and to explain less, than it once did. Regardless of the bad times they produce, cities still imply the possibility of a common life, even if only in its nostalgic absence, which makes them different from the informational privacy of suburbia, where the news may be on twenty-four hours a day, but where the sum of events never equates to a sense of greater belonging.

"In these years," Russell Banks has written, in *Continental Drift*, his novel of immigration and loss, ". . . most events and processes that have been occurring for millennia continue to occur." The problem, he says, is that the mediating script of history no longer writes us into reconciliation with the outside world, or with each other:

> We measure the geological change in millimeters per annum, feel nothing move beneath our feet and conclude, therefore, that nothing has happened. By the same token . . . because each new day brings a surfeit of . . . news, blotting out the news of the day before . . . we conclude here, too, that nothing has happened . . . so that, from birth to death, it seems to us who are caught in the beat of our own individual human hearts that everything happening on this planet is what happens to us, personally, privately, secretly. (41–42)

In his remarkable novel Banks gives voice to this sense of individuality turned to dread; in less eloquent terms, this same foreboding isolation makes otherwise improbable enterprises such as Niki's seem desirable and appealing. Middle-class individuals now confront a city that they and their parents made, or else imagine they made, but which the majority find hostile, unlivable, *other*. Its "history" is still present, in buildings and streets and municipal institutions—maybe the old neighborhood, even the house where you grew up—but that history no longer describes a home, which is where entrepreneurs like Niki come in. He and his fellow merchants offer what great numbers of people apparently want and need and are willing to pay for. Instead of being humiliated by a past that appears antagonistic and isolating—at once threatening, but also distinctly *ours*, as the present will never be—they undertake a secondary, reciprocal humiliation: they domesticate the past by humiliating it back, by packaging it as sociable, commercial pastiche.

## IV

The centerpiece of Niki's neighborhood is a gaudy piece of fakery called "Trapper's Alley," opened in 1985, in an enclosed mini-mall comprised of several nineteenth-century brick structures. There is no alley, but there are—or once were—trappers; they came here to sell their pelts and hides to Traugott Schmidt, who emigrated from Germany in 1852. That historic recollection provides the organizing theme of this "festival market," as it is subtitled. But the history so opportunely thematized is purely generic and might apply equally well to almost any American city, a point the developers—Cordish Embry & Associates—have been quick to capitalize elsewhere. The place, with its exposed red brick and brass reproduction fittings, merely stands for *pastness* as such. Nothing locates it in *this* city; nothing connects it to events specifically and uniquely defining of Detroit, any more than the products sold in the shops.

Aside from the usual fast-food outlets—Popeye's Fried Chicken, Sbarro's Pizza—there's the Purple Store, with its stock of cheap items, all of which are colored purple; or there's the little novelty boutique, Lefties Corner, specializing in T-shirts and mugs that sloganeer on behalf of left-handedness. Across the way is Get Sauced, where the inventory consists of improbable and high-priced condiments: tiny bottles of Nervous Nellie Hot Pepper Jelly for $6.95 or Blueberry Chutney for $7.95. There are also obscene greeting cards, scented oils or sticks of incense, and tiny crystals on simulated gold chains; and Corry the Psychic will provide a reading. These are not the kinds of retailers that typically show up in suburban malls, where shopping is more directly tied to necessity. In contrast, most products here are meant as jokes. Which puts an odd spin on the notion of renewal: the city once stood for an urbane, commercial superiority; now it is represented by little imported souvenirs that memorialize the inconsequence of time spent in urban space. Only a single T-shirt vendor has kept the faith. Fit To A Tee is still committed to history, after a fashion; there you can buy a shirt imprinted to mimic a dictionary definition: "Detroit n /di-troit'/ Fr détroit, strait): 1. Industrial city in s.e. Michigan where the weak are killed and eaten."

The conversion of Trappers Alley has generally called for the erasure of such powerful, if ridiculous, impressions. While the space appears to be historical, it happily imposes none of the burdens (or threats) that a still untranscended past might entail. This is precisely what is meant by its designation as "festival marketplace," and what makes it the unofficial city hall of Greektown. Here, the past gets interpreted as a perpetual carnival, which is just the opposite of history. Within this space, the nostalgia for history can be shared, just as city life once was, but the experience is purely recreational: a holiday interruption, a freak. This is nowhere more obvious than at The Fudgery, where a staff of black teenagers nightly put on an a cappella doo-wop show while they prepare the fudge, slapping great blobs of the gooey stuff down onto marble slabs for shaping. These are the same menacing kids of urban crime statistics and suburban paranoia, now fully domesticated. They—or the parties responsible for this popular performance—turn racial difference into a smiling entertainment option, rather than something real and troubling and not to be joked away.

The unrequited homelessness that such projects pander to and profit from is what marks the real difference between Niki and his suburban visitors. He *chose* to become an alien, urged on by innocent (if canny) dreams. And in that he simply followed the example of countless others before him, who went off looking to found their own particular "City Upon a Hill." That seems, more or less, to have been what Antoine Laument had in mind when he entered the service of Louis XIV and ended up inventing both himself and Detroit, which he first called *Fort Pontchartrain du Détroit*, in commemoration of the fort's location on a strait (*détroit*), and of his patron, Count Pontchartrain. Once he arrived here, out of reach of his superiors, the hardscrabble Laument translated himself into the gentility of Antoine de la Mothe, Sieur de Cadillac. "Cadillac" made it happen, just as Niki would later do, only a few blocks from the spot where the founder planted his flag. Each man turned homelessness to social credit and found among strangers a fortune to be made. But this matter of choosing to become an alien separates Niki and Cadillac from native residents who discover they have no hometown to return to, except in the contrived spaces of entrepreneurs. It's not opportunity these people sense, but something else.

This possibly explains the contradictory attitude Americans have toward their cities. Although fewer than a third of the population are still found there (32 percent), fewer still think of cities as the most desirable place to live (13 percent). At the same time, however, 79 percent think that saving the cities should be a key priority of the federal government. This means that virtually the same percentage of people who find cities undesirable places to live (87 percent) believe simultaneously that those places should be saved (79 percent) (Morgenthau 42). It is no longer sufficient, then, to think only in terms of material or demographic actuality or purely rational categories. Although most people choose to live elsewhere, they haven't been able to abandon the city imaginatively, whether out of nostalgia or guilt or a combination of the two. The city, therefore, is not so much a place, or even a memory, as it is a complex figure in which past and present are always overlaid and contending. And this figure, precisely because of its ambiguity, is not likely to resolve itself into a settled, unitary meaning, which is a truth at once made obvious by Niki's unexceptionable sign.

## V

Nobody could have guessed Niki's sign because it wasn't really made, in any usual sense; it was arrived at. The sign is a complex assemblage that becomes visible right out in front of the Taverna, where large glass windows come into opposition, meeting at an angle of about a hundred degrees with doors at the points of intersection. The panes are old, with slight undulations in their surface. On the left red and white letters spell out Niki's name. Business got so good on that side of the building that he decided to expand; he bought out the bakery next door, knocked down the interior walls, and doubled the size of his operation. The deal probably didn't cost much because the Acropolis, as the bakery was called, had never become a success. The Greeks who owned it didn't speak much

English and seemed only interested in doing business with other Greeks. So Niki came easily by his extra space, and also the rest of his sign, which didn't emerge until after he had scraped the competition's impermanent signature off the neighboring glass. Then, a wonderful thing happened. The history Niki was so busily (and successfully) humiliating signed itself—surreptitiously—right on the window of his restaurant, which is doubtless why it was allowed to stay. Once the Acropolis disappeared, another and much older sign became visible: "Dodge Brothers." That's what the sign says. Or rather that's what the faint impressions, left on the glass surface, can be seen to spell out, if you get the light just right.

The brothers referred to are John and Horace Dodge, founders of the automobile company that still bears their name. The Boydell Building, as Niki's place on Beaubien Street was then called, housed their machine shop from 1901 until some time in 1903, when they put up a bigger plant a couple of blocks east on Monroe at Hastings. It was here at Niki's, though, that they made their first great success; they built engines and transmissions for Ransom Olds's "Merry Oldsmobiles" after his own factory burned down. More important, this is likely the place where the brothers met Henry Ford, for whom they contracted to produce the running gear of the Model A, the car that would make all three of them rich men. Ford had only an idea at the time. He lacked either a factory or capital, and the assembly line had not yet been thought of. He'd already failed in two previous ventures, so backing of any sort was hard to arrange. His success depended on John and Horace—men like Niki, who had come to town to invent things and who brought with them a gambler's nerve. The result of their gamble is well known; it is no less surely, if ambiguously, inscribed on the face of this city than John and Horace's letters remain inscribed on Niki's glass, almost a hundred years after the brothers moved out.

Like those transparent impressions, which are the only memorial to the famous brothers' tenancy, the city itself has been rendered similarly transparent: deprived of the historical presence—the cultural paint between the lines—that once preserved this place against vandalism and looting by signing the fact of specific habitation.

Abandonment now becomes the justification for the precise acts of stripping—actual as well as metaphoric—that fulfill the prophecy already scripted for Detroit: America's first urban domino to fall. The city, then, in its popular representations, is apropos of nothing so much as expediency: a general need to imagine the worst but to imagine it as both titillatingly close and at the same time exotically distant.

Which is how Detroit came to be on the cover of the Sunday *Times* magazine, along with Ze'ev Chafets, author of *Devil's Night and Other True Tales of Detroit.* Chafets is an Israeli journalist who returned after twenty years to a "hometown" he never actually lived in, to record otherwise unremarkable and mostly unhappy "tales" of urban life—tales of poverty, racial hatred, degradation, abandoned hopes, death. Given what Americans now know about cities, these stories—even ones involving the ritualized arson of "Devil's Night," which gives the book its title—would remain sadly unextraordinary, except for their being "true tales of Detroit." As the jacket blurb breathlessly informs readers,

> In capturing Devil's Night and other troubling Motown movements, Ze'ev Chafets—hailed as a "1980s de Tocqueville" by *The New York Times*—returns to the city of his youth. . . . *Devil's Night: And Other True Tales of Detroit* gives an unprecedented look at what Ze'ev Chafets calls "America's first Third World City."

The blurb—like the book—fairly represents the fascination of "tourists, sociologists, even some visiting firefighters" (not to mention Chafets himself, as well as the *New York Times*) with the spectacle of an abandoned citizenry humiliating their lives and town of meaning, which is perhaps what Americans have come to expect of the Third World, and Detroit.

But if Detroit were simply a domestic "Third World City," as Chafets proposes, and as he and his readers would doubtless like to believe, then there would probably be no greater interest—or sales potential—than in most things relating to the Third World. But this is a Third World City that *we*—not *they*—made. Its degradation, therefore, humiliates not only the physical remains "we" left behind, but it also implicates the cultural pretensions on which "our" superiority and insight are founded. This may be why Detroit presents so frightful, yet irresistible, a challenge. The perpetual *othering* of this place—the consigning of its too familiar terrors to another world—makes it possible not only to evade responsibility for our own worst fears, but also, perhaps more crucially, it preserves for us the belief that our culture does not carry within it those seeds of death, which are come to such terrible fruition here.

## VI

Figure and ground, and the power of names: The celebrated Model A wasn't really a Ford at all; it was a Dodge engine and chassis, underneath a Wilson carriage body, assembled piecemeal by workers paid with other men's money. But Henry had the sense to name it and to stamp his figure on the radiator, though even that, the famous Ford ellipse, was another man's doing as well. No matter: even after he has been seen through, Henry is no less real; nor is the "Renaissance City" that middle-class evacuation has made it possible—literally—to see through. The city is neither one thing nor the other, neither the empty dark places nor the shiny restored ones; it is both at once, back and forth: a kind of monumental gestalt puzzle. It would be difficult to write a history based on a figure such as that, however, because narratives—even postmodern ones—still operate only one line at a time, left to right, just as they always have. Perhaps the history that comes *after* middle-class culture can only be gotten at by other means, as in Niki's remarkable signs, each of which, in its own way, is there both to signify and also to be seen through.

But that—the seeing through things—is just the problem because the more transparent the city becomes, the more official practitioners of information—journalists, correspondents, politicians, interpreters of all sorts—want to tell stories about it, as if to preserve the instruments of their knowledge against the threat of overthrow. Like gawkers assembling at an accident scene, where the urge is to see the worst, and by looking upon disaster to gain mastery over it, the level of coverage becomes an indicator of dread. But the more stories that get told, the less relevant storytelling seems to the task at hand. No matter how true the tales may be—as accounts of people or places or things—they end up like other historic markers; they stand for a kind of memory that nobody who lives here still looks to for explanations.

This is no longer the narrative common ground once (upon a time) projected by the middle class. Consequently, the history that's relevant is not likely to be comprehended in linear, story-keeper's terms: "Right now the failure of our families is hurting America deeply. When families fail, society fails. The anarchy and lack of structure in our inner cities are testament to how quickly civilization falls apart when the family foundation cracks" (Quayle A11). Though it is undoubtedly true that the health of a society and the health of the families that make it up are intimately related, Vice President Quayle's version of the city (apropos of the Los Angeles riots) dangerously ignores the facts. His ignorance is perhaps excusable or at least understandable and typical, however, because we have yet to devise a replacement for narrative as a means of comprehension. Violence becomes explicable, then, because families have failed, because civilization falls apart. Run these stories backwards, and they become a script for urban renewal and also a warrant for coercion: People must be made to do the right thing. But where is the city that honors narrative contracts, where the truth is indemnified by a storyteller's faith in the cumulative value of time? That city no longer exists; its history—now—consists in the piecemeal devaluation of precisely those forms of memory and attention.

Which point Niki has made clear in his appropriation of the Dodge Brothers' old machine shop. His historic restoration, like most others, didn't restore anything at all; on the contrary, it mocks the precise failure of narrative production that makes Detroit so ambiguous a symbol of humiliated American pride, Lee Iacocca notwithstanding. Niki restored the abandoned space on Beaubien, where nobody wants to make cars any more, by translating the visible signs of dereliction into valorizing props. The exposed brick walls, the old shop floors, the outmoded industrial fittings, all testify to the authenticity of his anachronistic enterprise; they vouch for the quality of his improbable—if famous—"square Greek pizzas" offered up in this museum of abandonment. Patrons pay happily for the privilege of condescending to a past made to seem comfortingly exotic and therefore no longer implicated in their lives and fates.

And out front, keeping track of all that goes on, is the sign, where those panes of plate glass angle in toward each other to form a self-regarding *V*. Each one glances humiliation back at the other, with the all-but-invisible Dodge Brothers reflecting on the pizza man's prideful self-inscription. Despite all the seeing through that goes on, it would be wrong, however, to assume that this place, or the supposedly postmodern visitors in it, exist beyond, or outside, of history, regardless of what they buy, or say, or do. No matter how far people move away, in other words, they are still moving—back and forth—on behalf of the city and what we have made of it. But the history that is relevant and determining, now, and the forms that it comes—without excuses—in, are not ones easily reduced to text. Instead, it is at places like Niki's, where the past is simultaneously restored and effaced, honored and humiliated, that things—however briefly—become clear. And that is why the most humiliated of cities is also the most representative: because it has endured, more than any other, what we have made of history; because it has been the most seen through. For the same reason, it is also the city that becomes the hardest, finally, to know.

## VII

So you look through Niki's windows, and the letters painted on them, and there everyone is: tourists (even if they happen to be natives), eating square pizzas, served by a Greek, in a retro-fitted room, in a building on Beaubien Street that the Dodge Brothers used to rent, where the first Fords got their start, in this made-up "town," part of a city the French invented and the British took away and "we" finally inherited, and then abandoned to "them," that nobody calls *Détroit* any more. Here we all are: the people seen through the glass; the figures written on the glass, figures being seen through in order to see them, the people; and the image of the spectator, perhaps there, in the glass, reflected. Each of these signifying agents embarked on mutually unintelligible errands, each resident of a different moment, ideologically and culturally. But they all, simultaneously, converge here, in the city, overlaid in a figure that both honors the past and also humiliates it, just as it humiliates us. Niki's windows know more about Detroit, then, and what has become of history in this most representative of American towns than any account people are likely to invent—my own included, I hasten to add.

# Coverage

## Coverage or the Fire Next Door? The Middle Class after Culture

*The city does not consist of this, but of relationships between the measurements of its space and the events of its past . . . . The city, however, does not tell its past, but contains it like the lines of a hand, written in the corners of the streets, the gratings of the windows, the banisters of the steps, the antennae of the lightning rods, the poles of the flags, every segment marked in turn with scratches, indentations, scrolls.*

—Italo Calvino

### I: The Fire

Coverage or the fire next door? Which is to be preferred? The choice is decisive. But thanks to the apparently seamless working-out of things, it's only by accident that anybody ever notices a real question being asked, or an answer being given. Even so, the not-having-to-choose hasn't made people, particularly middle-class people, feel any more at home with the cities they have built. Just the reverse.

Coverage or the fire next door? I came upon the question honestly, by accident. A friend had offered me a ride home from work, as she often does, so we got in her car and started the short trip downtown, toward the old center of the city where my apartment is (or where it was then). Usually she'd drop me off in front of my building, but today that was impossible. She couldn't even come close because of the police barricades blocking various intersections.

I got out of the car and started walking, wondering vaguely why the streets had been cordoned off. And also wondering why there were so many other people here. Even though I lived in the "heart" of downtown—as this neighborhood is sometimes called, rather out of nostalgia than a respect for demographic fact—it's rare to meet more than an occasional pedestrian on the streets, except at lunch, or at 5:00, when the offices close and the secretaries and government workers go home. It was only just past 4:00 now, and still quite a few people were out. Not many of them looked like office workers, however. They were neighborhood folks mostly—old people, delivery boys, spare change hustlers, homeless men and women who usually spend the afternoon slumped in doorways or else arguing with invisible hangers-on. But today everybody was up and moving, and heading in the same direction I was, for reasons yet to become apparent.

Our destination didn't remain a puzzle for long, though. Pretty soon I began to smell something burning. And then I saw a fireman go running down an alley up ahead. Even from two blocks away I could hear, and feel, the thudding of the diesel pumper engines. Then, rounding a corner, I saw a tall plume of black smoke, and a couple of minutes later, I could see the fire. The building that was burning was quite large, seven stories tall and a full city block wide; it had once been an exclusive department store for ladies back before anyone might have suspected that the city—least of all this part—would ever find itself in need of renewal. "Himelhochs, Woodward Thru to Washington," the chic, full-page advertisement reads in *The Social Secretary* for 1924, "Individual Apparel for Every Social Occasion at the Himelhoch Shops: *Gowns, Wraps, Millinery, Accessories*" (6). In the accompanying illustration a stylized flapper casts a languid glance at the reader through half closed eyes; she's disdainful and perfectly *smart*, as Scott Fitzgerald might have said. The Himelhoch brothers built their store in the years right after the First World War, when most of the rest of downtown took on its present shape. Or rather, the shape it had when people still launched their "occasions" with supplies that came from here. That was a long time ago. The building on fire hadn't been a store for years. First, for quite a while, it hadn't been anything at all except empty, which is what most structures on this once fashionable boulevard still are. Then, after abandonment and various bankruptcies had made downtown real estate fire-sale cheap, the erstwhile carriage-trade emporium was converted into rent-subsidized apartments for senior citizens, many of whom are now teetering uncertainly on the sidewalk out in front while they watch their belongings burn.

In front of my own building, which is next door, a reporter from the local NBC affiliate is conducting live interviews. Her video man is shooting low angle stuff with the fire—I expect—making a fine, dramatic backdrop. She's interviewing the manager of my building now; in his enthusiasm, he keeps turning toward Himelhoch's, pointing and gesturing, telling her what's going on. The reporter, who grasps him firmly by the elbow, out of frame, has to be swiveling him constantly back around to face the camera. It's obvious she's had experience with amateur eye witnesses. Off camera, to the left, there's a little queue of people waiting their turn to be interviewed: the afternoon doorman from my building, the barber from around the corner, a UPS delivery man, whose truck is double parked in front. There's plenty of noise and action out here on the street, but the mood is businesslike: a bunch of trained people are just doing their jobs. I take another look at the fire and then go inside.

In the elevator, riding up to my floor, I think of the time my parents got me out of bed to go and watch the Thornton store burn. I was six, and Thornton's was the biggest and oldest department store in the small Texas town where I grew up. I remember standing across the street with my parents and several hundred other people. It seemed like the middle of the night to me, but it was probably only 9:00 or 10:00 p.m. We stood there, I expect, for several hours, but I don't remember wanting to leave. The store was three or four stories and must have been the biggest building in town at the time, right across from the courthouse. It was surely the grandest, with hardwood floors, Corinthian columns, an opulent mezzanine, and the first escalator I'd ever seen: "a city within itself," as the boastful advertising slogan proclaimed. The whole fire department had probably been called out, but there was no stopping that blaze. Thornton's block had been assembled from a collection of smaller buildings in the first years of the century, on the very site of old E. L. Thornton's general store. That was long before there were laws about sprinkler systems and fire retardant construction materials. The outside was brick, and withstood the blaze pretty well, but the wood interior went up like tinder.

Standing there, watching the fire, I felt as if we were all waiting for something more to happen, though I didn't know what: some cosmic acknowledgment of the catastrophe taking place. Then all at once the mezzanine collapsed, which made a great, wrenching noise and sent sparks shooting up through the burned-out roof like in the cartoons I was fond of when somebody blew their top. My parents and I waited until the fire was out, or mostly out. I don't remember our talking much, except for my father's saying he was worried about a sterling silver tea set he'd bought but not picked up. He was president of the PTA, and they'd decided to get the tea set for a first-grade teacher, Miss Heathington, who was retiring after fifty years. My father was worried that the store might not make good his purchase.

What the Thorntons did—not the "old man," but his sons—was to take some of their insurance money and build two suburban stores, in addition to buying my father a second tea service. They rebuilt the old store too, but as everybody said, it just wasn't the same. Then a couple of years later, my family followed the sons out of downtown, away from the neighborhood where I and my mother had both been born, and where her parents had settled right after they got married in 1906. My father bought a new house in the suburbs, just as the fathers of most of my friends were doing, and we went to live in a cotton field, on a street that extended no further than the end of our block. Now, thirty years later, there's no trace left of the cotton field, or the woods that once surrounded it; and the street—like the suburbs—continues on for miles beyond what was once my house at the edge of town. As for me, I have done what a lot of other people my age are doing: I have traveled a great circle route back to where I started out.

But I'm not precisely back where I was: the familial journey that began at ground level, in my grandfather's house downtown, has ended up in the air, in a city much larger and older than the one where he lived, which is where I am now. The elevator stops at my floor, and I walk down the hall to my apartment. I let myself in, drop my briefcase on the sofa, and without thinking a great deal about what I'm doing, go into the bedroom and turn on the TV. As I wait for the picture to appear, I look out the window, toward the street, where I can see the reporter, who is now talking to my doorman. And, as I glance toward the TV, there they are on the screen too. A trailer runs across the bottom explaining that this is an "Action Newsbrief"; in the upper right corner of the picture, there is imprinted the word *LIVE*, with a clock below, ticking off the digitalized minutes as they pass. I turn up the sound and hear the doorman saying that the fire looks under control. Then there's a cut to the Eye-in-the-Sky helicopter that I can hear hovering overhead. I look up, out my window, and there it is, and there on the TV, looking up, I can see myself watching it looking down.

What I discover, unintentionally, when the building next door caught fire is that the fire itself seems not nearly so absorbing as the coverage of the fire, which is why people wait in line to tell a reporter what everybody present already knows, and why the reporter bothers to ask them in the first place. While there's no denying the fire, or that some people will be permanently affected by it, such information is of little relevance, unless you happen to be one of those unfortunate individuals. It is not the fire, then, but the fact that the fire is being covered that makes these events worth watching. That's why we all stay tuned. This puts us inside a different moment entirely from the one my parents and I inhabited when we stood watching the old Thornton's burn. Then, it was inconceivable that an event so central to civic culture should take place without being witnessed directly, personally. You would want to have seen it yourself so you could tell other people you had been there. Now, it's hard to imagine what an event central to civic culture might be, the L.A. riots notwithstanding; and it's even harder to imagine the conditions under which the fractured inconvenience, and danger, of firsthand spectatorship would be preferable to the completer coverage available at home.

## II: AfterCulture

At 11:00, when the news comes on, it starts the same way on each of the three network affiliates. There's a swirl of computer generated graphics announcing the name of the report and giving the relevant channel number, and then through the titles there emerges a nighttime location shot, which (allowing for local variations) is the same, whether it's this city whose news is about to be reported, or some other. The high-altitude camera eye rushes with dizzying speed toward the illuminated downtown and then, at an even faster rate, zooms in at the very center of the tall buildings, as if drawn there by the intense, gravitational pull of events. What's interesting about this visual display is that the location cited bears little relation to the station doing the reporting and even less to the origin of the news that follows, or the lives of the people who are watching it. In Detroit, for example, only one of the three network affiliates even retains a studio in town, and that one is not located where the camera eye ends up looking. Nor is the majority of viewers to be found here, any more than the work that sustains their lives. Of the three to four million people in the metropolitan area, only a million actually live inside the city limits. The rest are to be found in a loosely related confederation of suburbs, the only common feature of which is a shared wish *not* to be part of the city.

That degree of displacement may be extreme, but the pattern is similar in most big cities, and typical of America generally, where the majority of our formerly urban population is no longer urban at all, which was obvious even before the 1990 census began: "The 1980 census revealed that more than 40 percent of the national population, or more than 100 million people, lived in the suburbs, a higher proportion than resided either in rural areas or in central cities" (Jackson 4). Given the new affiliations that have grown up, between the places that people call home these days and the center cities that most of them live near (though no longer in), the term "suburb" itself is probably outmoded. As Nicholas Lemann noted recently in the *Atlantic*,

> People's concept of suburbia, like their concepts of summer and marriage, comes more from what they knew growing up than from what they've experienced themselves as adults. . . . While we've been glorifying the suburbs of the fifties, the suburbs of the eighties have been evolving into places quite different. The most obvious change has been a political-economic one: in the fifties the suburbs were exclusively residential, but businesses have been moving to them over the past fifteen years, and this has broken the iron association of suburbs with commuting downtown. (34)

In this respect too, my city is typical, so that a television station interested in accurately representing its constituency would begin the news—particularly as it pertains to middle-class viewers—with a sweeping panorama of the the ex-urban necklace that adorns the outer rim of the town, with intermittent (and haphazard) conglomerations of office towers, hotel/restaurant complexes, apartment "villages," and strip malls. That's where the majority of residents live and work and consume these days; and it has nothing to do with downtown.

But that's not the site from which the news originates—at least it is not the informational stage on which that news is set. Instead of instancing the decentered "technoburbs" (Lemann 34) that are now the basis of middle-class life, the news enacts a nightly eternal return, playing out an absentee fantasy of origins. First the city made the middle class possible, and then it made them want to move away, though not (at least initially) for reasons of avoidance so much as a wish to translate material prosperity into a place of their own:

> The *total* number of housing units in the United States has doubled since the [Second World] war, thus changing the very nature of everyday life as the American family deconcentrated into a small nuclear group housed in single-family homes. . . . Furthermore, the

> placement of such [homes] almost overwhelmingly occurs in the suburban sections of our metropolitan regions. (Gottdiener 242)

In this town, for example, three-quarters of the populace have traditionally lived in individual houses, which has meant a constant need for more and more space. Sooner or later, that need (combined with the city's inability and/or refusal to grow) led to the proliferation of postwar suburbia, and then ex-urbia. But even after distance and poverty and crime and racism have finally rendered great parts of the city itself no longer desirable, as an actual residence, its *idea* persists, perhaps even grows more powerful, which accounts for the replacement of a genuine urban culture with the fantasized coverage of TV.

"When a man rides a long time through wild regions," Calvino wrote in his *Invisible Cities*, "he feels the desire for a city" (8). Now, perhaps more than ever, people desire the imagined consolation of the city: after the long ride out toward the suburbs, and beyond; after the historical evacuation of the place they remember as their *home* town. We have been traveling through "wild regions," like that cotton field my family landed in, or like the synthetic technoburbs that ring the city where I live now, so that the idea of town takes on a power that only separation—absence—can endow. "While we are losing a lot of functions that we used to enjoy [in cities]," William H. Whyte, author of *The Organization Man*, recently told *Time* magazine, "we are intensifying the most important function of all—a place for coming together" (Allis 9). But in many places, I suspect—surely it is true of the one where I live—the "coming together" is still more a matter of abstractions, such as the images projected by an evening news show, than it is of actual relocation. Precisely because cities have lost "a lot of functions that we used to enjoy" they seem unnecessary, incomprehensible, and forbidding, except as nostalgic fantasies—"invisible" metropolises, as Calvino said.

And perhaps more than to any other group, they seem this way to the class whose culture, historically, is the product of institutions the dissolution of which becomes the defining feature of contemporary urban space. It was not for the working classes that the great "cultural" apparatus of the city was invented. They lacked both the leisure and the money to support such extravagance. This is the dispiriting lesson that Dreiser's Carrie Meeber soon learns, for example, when she joins her hard-driving sister in Chicago: "Minnie's manner was one of trained industry, and Carrie could see that it was a steady round of toil with her. . . . The whole atmosphere of the flat [implied] a settled opposition to anything save a conservative round of toil" (18). This settled opposition of Minnie's, while considered a virtue in a working woman, specifically prohibits the education that enables Carrie to rise in the world. Until she escapes her sister's house and way of life, Carrie cannot avail herself of the social and commercial instruction that the city offers—instruction that she will need if she is ever to become middle class.

Dreiser brings Carrie to Chicago in 1889; at virtually the same time, the popular novelist William Dean Howells undertook a fictional move parallel to his personal change of residence. In *A Hazard of New Fortunes*, he brings two of his most successful previous characters, Basil and Isabel March, from Boston—a city associated with the traditions of America's colonial past—to New York —a city associated with its commercial future. Faced with the prospect of such a move, Isabel, who is a native Bostonian, makes the following objections to her husband: "'I could go West with you,'" she says, "'or into a new country—anywhere; but New York terrifies me. . . . I can't find myself in it; I shouldn't know how to shop'" (1976: 28). Of necessity, the "new" cities of America—cities like New York, and Chicago, and St. Louis, and Detroit—assumed the didactic burden implicit in Isabel's characterization: they instituted a commercial culture to take the place of actual memory and association. The city taught anonymous arrivistes such as the Marches how to spend their money and time and so "find themselves" in association with other like-minded people. Working women like Carrie's sister Minnie lacked the leisure for such instruction, and "old money" families either disdained contact with the overt didacticism of popular institutions or else had servants to do the shopping for them. But the people in the middle—people like Basil and Isabel—benefited by the city's institutionalized willingness to instruct. And as Isabel's complaint suggests, perhaps the most exemplary forms of instruction were devoted to shopping—specifically the sort of shopping introduced in the department store.

Such establishments embody the essence of middle-class, urban culture. They institutionalize and democratize the solution to Isabel's question: For at least four generations, they translated money (regardless of how recently, or variously, made) into the visible, and communicable, signs of a uniform "culture." To that end, the store became self-consciously didactic, as evident in the "Marshall Field & Company Idea," first published by the store in 1905, for the benefit of its employees, whom it instructed:

> To do the right thing at the right time, in the right way; to do some things better than they were ever done before; to eliminate errors; to know both sides of the question . . . to be an example . . . to act for reason rather than rule; to be satisfied with nothing short of perfection. (Birmingham 183)

Access to such exemplary establishments as Field's was crucial, which accounts for both their centralized locations and ready adoption of the latest technology: pneumatic billing systems, time payments, elevators, escalators, and so on. At J. L. Hudson's, for example, which was the main department store in Detroit, by 1911 there were fifty passenger elevators in addition to escalators and various stairs. The middle-class culture of opportunity, plenitude, and upward mobility represented abstractly by the city became a material fact inside the store. (Like the other major downtown retailers—Crowley's, Kern's—J. L. Hudson did not advertise in the *Social Register* of 1924, doubtless on the presumption that his appeal was to customers still on their way up, rather than the ones who had already arrived.)

That cities, and the situation of the class historically created by them, now seem so puzzling and often threatening may have a lot to do with the vanishing of institutions that once made sense out of them—institutions offering a culture (regardless of how apparently exclusionary now), which proposed to stand for the whole: "to know both sides of the question, to be an example, to be satisfied with nothing short of perfection." Very little is left of that culture these days:

> The decay of the central city continues—its revenue base eroded by the retreat of industry and white middle-class families to the suburbs, its budget and tax rate inflated by rising costs and increasing numbers of dependent citizens and its public plant schools, hospitals and correctional institutions deteriorated by age and long deferred maintenance. (*Report of the National Advisory Commission* 283–84)

The conclusions of the so-called Kerner Commission were published following the urban riots of the late sixties; nothing has happened in the interim to reverse the trends already then clearly established.

"It had taken Abdul Karim years to sort out the city," Thomas Glynn writes in *The Building* (1986), his hallucinogenic allegory of New York: "When he first arrived he was struck by the magnificence and decay. Why should the richest city on earth, the richest city history had ever seen, allow itself to crumble?" (21). Glynn's New York is paradigmatic of most other, older cities in their combination of "magnificence and decay," and subject, likewise, to Abdul Karim's explanation. Why does the city allow itself to crumble? "The reason, he now knew, was because of a plot" (21). The plot that carried people into town—the plot that novelists like Howells and Dreiser elaborated in such detail—has now carried them back out of it. The story of the good life is no longer being written and read at metropolitan institutions—schools, stores, parks, theaters—which end up as decaying last resorts for the people who can't afford anything better. The city is still here, of course, in a physical sense; and thousands of people continue to live in this space that exists after the withdrawal of middle-class culture. But mere persistence doesn't make the remains, whether human or architectural, seem any more attractive or comprehensible to outsiders who happen upon a past that their own moving out of it has created.

In Detroit, for example, the downtown Hudson's—which was our Macy's or Dayton's or Marshall Field's—closed in the mid-1980s, after a lengthy period of decline. (It was soon followed by the remaining large retailers, F. W. Woolworth, and even S. S. Kresge's store number one, first of the chain that became K-Mart.) Everybody simply followed the demographics out of downtown. The enormous red-brick Hudson's building remains, vacant, although developers claim to have plans for a multipurpose reinhabitation. Such stories are reported frequently, with little conviction, in the local newspapers, along with Elvis sightings, but none has ever amounted to anything more than that—a story. The formerly self-explanatory city, which used to want to teach people things about culture, now shows a sad neglect of its various schools, particularly the public ones. As a consequence, the best things the town still has to offer are either more or less private these days, from schools to urban mini-malls, with their boutique-style shops and carefully controlled access. Security becomes an inevitable concern because the carefully plotted discipline of culture is no longer available to act *in loco* the cops.

This means that the city, ironically, retains something of its representational value, even yet; it produces an inverted version of the plot that abandonment has visibly deconstructed—at least with respect to the middle-class. Old American cities literalize the "fear of falling," as Barbara Ehrenreich has called it, that defines the end-point of middle-class culture—an end-point that has now been reached by substantial numbers of prosperous, thirtysomething adults:

> In the middle class there is another anxiety: a fear of inner weakness, of growing soft, of failing to strive, of losing discipline and will. Even the affluence that is so often the goal of all this striving becomes a threat, for it holds out the possibility of hedonism and self-indulgence. Whether the middle class looks down toward the realm of less, or up toward the realm of more, there is the fear, always, of falling. (15)

As Nicholas Lemann has pointed out with regard to the isolation that this "fear" invites, "middle-class Americans have gone from glorifying group bonding to glorifying individual happiness and achievement" (46)—an observation that is not precisely news. But what endows this final "triumph of the individual" (as John Naisbitt calls it, 1990: 298) with Ehrenreich's fear of falling is the recognition that the institutions of democratic culture are in a state of visible decay. They are no longer there to break the fall after culture. And this becomes nowhere more apparent, and frightening, than in the absent heart of America's great cities. There the combination of magnificence and decay is unmistakable, as Abdul Karim said, and along with it the loss of discipline, the failure of will, that make the spectacle both fearful and admonitory, and also profoundly isolating.

Still, this is where I have ended up, at the conclusion of a two-generation U-turn that began at my grandfather's house: one that has landed me, finally, here, up in the air, where I look down from the twenty-seventh floor (in a co-op I bought after I left my apartment in the building next door to the fire, which was five blocks away). I watch the afterlife of a city that he would have first known in its prime, and at ground level. This is where I have chosen to be, and the choice—at least statistically—is not an unusual one; it accounts for the several thousand reinhabitants of this city who live more or less as I do. (These are the same people who could be found reinhabiting the downtowns of most old American cities, the people who have made literal the nightly returns of the 11:00 news.) We are the source of a current mini-boom in high-rise renewals of previously abandoned urban space. It may have taken a long time to perfect the means of our elevation, architecturally as well as culturally, but these were in no sense unplanned or unexpected. It's where our desires were always tending.

Writing about the vertical afterculture that technology (and architecture) now makes available, Richard Sennett has remarked of this equivocal life that it is one

> in which sense data cannot be transmuted into social communication, a condition we can see in walking around the center of any modern city. Or more generously, we might say Mies [van der Rohe] converted into the most exquisite visual form the Romantic philosopher's fear of slavery, the slavery of being pent-up inside yet knowing the outer world, a prison without bars or even walls. . . . [W]hat does it matter that, far from being as advertised, the architecture inspired by plate glass draws us into the spiritual problems of an earlier age? . . . The practical problem of urban design now is how men and women can cope with the solitude imposed upon them by modernism. (1987: 7)

The answer, of course, is that they don't, at least not in any effective way, which is why the high-rise "perfection" of individuality has brought with it Ehrenreich's fear of falling. At the same time, there are compensations, security not being the least of these. From where I sit, looking out my window, I can see, at a distance, other men and women like me, in other buildings like mine, looking out their windows perhaps—windows located, in fact, in buildings that Mies planned, in a park designed specifically, in the name of urban renewal, for him to build those structures in. And all of us are here —or at least most of us, I expect—as a result of desires fulfilled. We've come back to look down at the town that our grandparents built and our parents abandoned for something better. And the view, especially after dark, is spectacular. As good as TV.

But there is a cost to be paid for living in the city after culture, the city that is now dangerous and abandoned at ground level: the cost of being "pent up inside yet knowing the outer world." The question is how to interpret the separations that secure our position. As Sennett points out, this modernist "fulfillment" would be unachievable except for the "plate glass" from which his essay takes its title. That—plate glass—is what allows me the comprehensive view that makes my monthly maintenance worth paying. And when it gets dark, the glass walls of my apartment play an amusing trick. The windows reflect my own image back, mirrorlike, but the image appears to float out into space, several feet in front of the building. I like the view from inside well enough, but I also like to imagine what things must look like from out there. Whatever the fear of falling, whatever the solitude imposed by the location, that view is the one we've all been waiting for—all of us, at least, who have lived through culture to get where we are. Which is why the television cameras rush down here every night: to remind us—regardless of where we may actually live—that the news is now originating from that long-awaited spot.

## III: City Works

But regardless of the trend that put the *u* in Yuppie—the urge of postsuburban sons and daughters to reinhabit formerly abandoned *urban* space—the majority of middle-class citizens prefers to limit returns to the comparative safety of the evening news, or else to visits that closely parallel it. "Residual belief in the importance of a central city keeps the place populated nine to five," according to an article on metropolitan "New Frontiers" in *Detroit Monthly*: "It all looks like a real city, but you still need people on the streets in the twenty-three hours surrounding lunch" (Barron 58). Because people so infrequently visit this city without citizens, when they do decide to come, they often complain of the trouble they have finding their way around downtown. Which is an odd thing to happen, particularly here.

Like many other old downtowns, this one is practically unavoidable, and relentlessly centered, at least with respect to the layout of streets, which inscribe in concrete the (once) univocal plot of urban culture. "There are few cities in the country which at rush periods of the day have more intense and concentrated street traffic," according to a report delivered at a city planning conference held here in 1915. And among the reasons for this is "the concentration by means of diagonal arteries at practically one point of all street traffic coming to and leaving the business center" (29), which is where Hudson's and Himelhoch's were, along with the hotels, theaters, and civic buildings that stood for urban life, one of which would later become my apartment next door to the fire. These days, there isn't much traffic down here, even at "rush periods," as *Detroit Monthly* suggests, but the plan that seemed such a detriment in 1915 was never changed, so that everything still converges at the same, accustomed point. Thus, the problem visitors have in finding downtown is not one of simple directions so much as it is of culture.

These days, the observation is frequently made—in both popular and professional contexts—that the city has become "unreadable" or else "unmappable." Summarizing a good deal of current scholarly and artistic reflection, William Sharpe and Leonard Wallock have offered the following characterization of attempts at "reading the city": "If literature has been attempting to wrest meaning from the city's junkyard of broken images, in the social sciences the struggle to put a name to the shape of the modern city has been even more pronounced. It has, in fact, provoked a crisis of language" (29). In short, it seems that history—for reasons now hotly debated—has rendered the city a no longer decipherable text, which—street plans notwithstanding—explains why people invariably get lost whenever they enter.

But a moment's reflection on the reality of urban space renders this metaphor of "reading" at once both inappropriate and also revealing. In a physical sense, this is still the same city that people used to complain of for being too centered, too intent upon its own municipal purpose. As to the ability of inhabitants to communicate with one another, or with outsiders who are lost, there is little evidence for the after-Babel projected by writerly models. It is doubtful that this, or any other city, is more diverse linguistically or cartographically than the supposedly readable metropolises of the first half of this century. Unquestionably, however, one thing has changed, and that is the way middle-class writers and academics *feel* about their relationship to the city, which is the difference that their textual models are actually communicating.

In the same way that Magritte's famous illustration is "not a pipe" but a picture of a pipe, the city-as-text is likewise a representation. In fact, the city is no more a text than the picture of the pipe is a real one. It is true, however, that the city can be textualized in order to suit the needs of a particular group. In this regard, it is no accident, perhaps, that the city comes to be based on language because increasingly language makes up the work of a managerial and professional class founded on an economy of information/service. As yet, traditional cultural institutions have not caught up with the altered nature of work, so that class itself becomes more a question than an answer—an unreadable text for which the afterculture of the city can be taken as a metaphor and also blamed as a cause.

The difference between *then* and *now* is immediately obvious—readable—as for example in Sinclair Lewis's novel *Babbitt.* When George F. Babbitt drives into Zenith, there is no question about the city or the man approaching it. And what is most important, there is no question about the readerly authority of narrative to render the truth of both:

> All the while he was conscious of the loveliness of Zenith. . . . He admired each district along his familiar route to the office: The bungalows and shrubs and winding irregular driveways of Floral Heights. The one-story shops on Smith Street, a glare of plate-glass and new yellow brick; groceries and laundries and drug-stores to supply the more immediate needs of East Side housewives. The market gardens in Dutch Hollow, their shanties patched with corrugated iron and stolen doors. Billboards with crimson goddesses nine feet tall advertising cinema films, pipe tobacco, and talcum powder. The old "mansions" along Ninth Street, S. E., like aged dandies in filthy linen; wooden castles turned into boarding-houses, with muddy walks and rusty hedges, jostled by fast-intruding garages, cheap apartment-houses, and fruit-stands conducted by bland, sleek Athenians. Across the belt of railroad-tracks, factories with high-perched water-tanks and tall stacks—factories producing condensed milk, paper boxes, lighting-fixtures, motor cars. Then the business center, the thickening darting traffic, the crammed trolleys unloading, and high doorways of marble and polished granite. It was big—and Babbitt respected bigness in anything; in mountains, jewels, muscles, wealth, or words. He was, for a spring-enchanted moment, the lyric and almost unselfish lover of Zenith. (28–29)

What is notable about this passage is that the city Babbitt drives through is no less contradictory (or inherently unreadable) than the contemporary city: like the place where I live, it combines magnificence and decay in equal portions, with shanty-town squalor and the subdivided former "mansions" being no less representative than the "glare of plate-glass" and the "doorways of marble and polished granite." What makes things different is Babbitt's unchallenged faith that the whole of what he sees is comprehended by a single intelligence—an intelligence of which he and his class are culturally representative. The time he spends in driving downtown conforms to their shared narrative of arrival. And even though his faith in the virtual intelligence of his class becomes the object of Lewis's satire, the novelist is no less committed than Babbitt to the notion that comprehension is both possible and necessary. Otherwise, the superior, ironic send-up of Babbitt's petty bourgeois attitudes would be impossible.

That is what separates *now* from *then*, and particularly with regard to the city, which (in the manner of Magritte's pipe that is not really a pipe) stands for something else: institutionalized, representative culture. It is not the existence of cities so much as the continued capability of a particular culture to discover in them signs of their own comprehensive power that is now in question. As Sharpe and Wallock point out, "Like language, the city is a system of signification dependent on certain fixed relations and shared values for its comprehensibility or 'interpretation.' But if the traditional functions of the city are displaced to other parts of a more homogeneously urbanized environment, then the effect will resemble the loss of semiotic apprehendibility that Derrida describes" (15). What they fail to consider, however, is the totalizing impulse inherent in their description and the relation it bears to social class. Derrida is not so much a reader of the city, in other words, as he is a concurrent product of experiences that have rendered problematical the middle-class projection of "certain fixed relations and shared values."

The notion that the city is a text—a text that owes it to *us* to be readable—is one that projects the unitary discipline of literacy specifically onto the highly differentiated (and frequently unlettered) urban space. This projection makes time—the time of education, the time of the sentence, the time of narrative culture generally—the putative, organizing economy of all experience whatever. We hold the city responsible, then, for giving us back the image of our own power over it. But this kind of time is not universal; on the contrary, it is special to a particular class and a particular moment in the history of that class. The literacy thus instituted was necessary to the consolidation of power in a managerial class whose tasks centered on rationalizing a complex productive apparatus. But is that same literacy useful now?

As the ironic send-up of *Babbitt* makes clear, the "point" of middle-class life is submission: individual submission to the external discipline and authority of culture. A too complete and shortsighted submission makes Babbitt a fool in Lewis's eyes, but it is not the discipline of culture as such that he criticizes. (Otherwise the martyrdom of Babbitt's aesthetic friend Paul wouldn't have been possible.) Rather, Lewis has contempt for the cheapness and dishonesty that prevent middle-class culture from becoming a *true* one. The author, no less than his character, reverences the time-honored, and time-honoring, discipline of personal growth. And he has no choice because he is writing from the experience of a class that depends for its existence not on inheritance (of capital, or of work), but on a body of skills that must be mastered individually, generation by generation: "The professional and managerial occupations have a guildlike quality. They are open, for the most part, only to people who have completed a lengthy education and attained certain credentials. The period of study and apprenticeship—which may extend nearly to mid-life—is essential to the social cohesion of the middle class" (Ehrenreich 13). The problem now is that the narrative contract of middle-class culture (to get a good job, get a good education) seems visibly to be breaking down. Inflation and plentiful credit make generally available entitlements that were formerly withheld for the few. At the same time, the skills (like the degrees) that once assured a "good" life seem now to pay only half the bills.

In that context, then, the supposedly unreadable city emerges as a vicious parody of what seems to have overtaken the once dependable map of middle-class culture. People get lost downtown—the downtown of *their own* city—the same way they get lost on their way to the life they had expected and worked toward, so that by the 1980s, stories about "downward mobility" had become a cliché: "For the first time in postwar America, a middle-level income no longer guaranteed what we have come to think of as a middle-class lifestyle. But the big news was that the 'middle class,' or more precisely, the middle range of income, was becoming ever more sparsely inhabited" (Ehrenreich 205). In this way too, then, the depopulated city seems to be parodying the condition of its once favored citizens. The economic base is no longer here, the important jobs are mostly elsewhere, like the best neighborhoods, so that the abandoned institutions of the city stand not for popular entitlement, but for the creeping aphasia that seems now to have overthrown our formerly communicable culture. And this at the precise moment when the future is to be entrusted—theoretically—to an information revolution. No wonder people grow fearful. Understandably, then, critics turn upon the representational apparatus of urban culture, both holding it responsible for what has gone wrong and also trying to shame it back into standing for something intelligible and real.

The urge for textual totalization (the conviction that the city is, or *ought to be*, a text) is symptomatic of some general fears: the suspicion that there's going to be less room in the middle class than there used to be, with some doing much better, but with many doing worse; this along with the fear that the instructions for success are getting much harder to read in the world after culture. (The progressive inaccessibility of private home ownership is merely one particularly powerful bit of evidence.) And now, after the cultural restraints of the past have been overcome—seen through—the difference between the one and the other, between moving up and falling down, will largely be a matter of individual, *private* intelligence. "The great unifying theme at the conclusion of the 20th century is the triumph of the individual," John Naisbitt proclaims in his best-selling update, *Megatrends 2000* (1990: 298). "The triumph of the individual signals the demise of the collective," he continues, in the same bubbly tone (1990: 299). This would be good news to Isabel March, perhaps, who might move wherever she wanted nowadays without having to worry about knowing how to shop. The collective supervision of culture is off, which means that you shop however you want—at the mall nearest you, for example. But for the most part, this liberation has not produced the elation of Naisbitt's popularization. Just the reverse.

And here too the city is implicated: it stands for the emptiness that its own failure seems to have brought about. Once people got up and out of its grasp, and on to a life of their own, they were free to do as they pleased. But that "triumph" has been purchased at the price of consolations no longer available. The city reciprocated the respect of individuals who submitted to it: urban institutions compensated with a communicable "culture" the isolation that remains necessarily the basis of middle-class life. Admittedly, writers at least since Sinclair Lewis have been poking fun at the shoddy cheapness of that culture. Even so, the getting over the city and all it stood for and the arrival at the "perfection" of suburbia and ex-urbia have not cured people of their desire for what they (perhaps incorrectly) imagine to have gone on in town. "When a man rides a long time through wild regions," as Calvino observed, "he feels the desire for a city." Thus the nostalgia for return, simultaneous with the horror people often feel when they do. Thus too the modern appetite for coverage.

## IV: Coverage

What the novel was to the city built of narrative time, coverage is to the space left after it. Novelists, at least since the eighteenth century, have projected onto the town the stories they wanted to believe it told about itself and their—along with their readers'—place in the civic plot. And for quite a while, and for great numbers of people, the fictional reciprocity worked, at least well enough for the invented agendas of middle-class arrival to begin to seem like natural truths. The familiarity of such narratives allows Sinclair Lewis so economically, and recognizably, to sketch a George Babbitt, for whom time spent in the city is the only sort of time worth having: "Our greatness," Babbitt explains at the annual dinner of the Real Estate Board:

> lies not alone in punchful prosperity but equally in that public spirit, that forward-looking idealism and brotherhood, which has marked Zenith ever since its foundation by the Fathers. We have a right, indeed we have a duty toward our fair city, to announce broadcast the facts about our high schools . . . our magnificent new hotels and banks and the paintings and carved marble in their lobbies; and the Second National Tower, the second highest business building in any inland city in the entire country. When I add that we have an unparalleled number of miles of paved streets, bathrooms, vacuum cleaners, and all the other signs of civilization; that our library and art museum are well supported and housed in convenient and roomy buildings; that our park-system is more than up to par, with its handsome driveways adorned with grass, shrubs, and statuary, then I give but a hint of the all-round unlimited greatness of Zenith! (154)

Babbitt so skillfully summons—and summarizes—the collective culture of his class that he has become a proverbial figure, a category, as per this entry from Webster's *Dictionary*: "Babbitt . . . a business or professional man who conforms unthinkingly to prevailing middle-class standards" (81). Babbitt represents the city, correctly, as a production, just like the people in it—the "regular" people, that is. And this is the aspect of urban culture he extolls, tying his description to the narrative agenda of progress, which defines both an individual and also a collective autobiography. "Boosters—Pep!" as he was fond of saying.

That Babbitt's city is gone—even in places where cities still "work"—is obvious. And in places where they don't, the absence is even more apparent. Consider, for example, the handsome old clock that used to hang on the corner of the "Kern Block" in downtown Detroit. The clock is still in its accustomed place, elevated (now) on a brass pole. But the rest of the block is just so much empty space—a space (unexpectedly) created at the precise point referred to by the city planner in 1915, where the "diagonal arteries" converge, concentrating there "all street traffic coming to and leaving the business center" (29). Fittingly enough, then, that became the point to define a central time for the narratively centered city. Nowadays, when the time changes to daylight saving, or when there's a power outage, nobody bothers to reset the hands of the clock. Not that it matters: it's been years since anybody arranged a meeting "under the Kern's clock." Unlike other parts of downtown, though, this area is still populated throughout the day. There are banks and offices, with the usual complement of workers and managers, and there are a good number of permanent residents, who have turned this formerly busy commercial center into a neighborhood once more, which it hadn't been for a hundred years.

People gather around the occasionally accurate clock at all hours. Some live in alleys and spend the afternoons sleeping on the benches out in front of the building that used to be the Detroit Savings Bank. Others have regular apartments, but come here just for company. A vendor of fruit and incense has set up a more or less permanent operation in the doorway of the shuttered B. Siegel Co., which had the lead, three-color ad in the 1924 *Social Secretary*: "The Store that Means *so* Much *to* Women" (1). Across the way, leaning against the J. L. Hudson building, or sheltering in its shade, a group of regulars—middle-aged men, mostly—play checkers and sometimes chess. They're presided over by a Belushi-like character with a graying beard who listens constantly to a radio installed in a Budweiser can. He's fond of buttons. "Try a virgin," his current one reads. Around sundown, the crowd gets younger. The old people go indoors, or else get out of the way, and bands of teenagers, mostly boys, come here to hang out and call back and forth to each other. There's a lot of noise sometimes, but generally the neighborhood stays pretty safe.

But this would never have gotten to *be* a neighborhood again except for the failure of the city that Babbitt imagined: the city of "all-round unlimited greatness" founded on his plot of centralized growth and middle-class prosperity. If people still invested the kind of time here—both real and imaginary—that the Kern's clock represented, then there wouldn't be any space for the present, haphazard resettlement of street people and elderly pensioners to occur in. Not that these are the only citizens to take advantage of the narrative evacuation of downtown. There's an up-scale side to the politics of space. As *Detroit Monthly* put it, "Residual belief in the importance of a central city keeps the place populated nine to five." Real estate is cheap, and tax breaks are easy to come by, so that this "residual belief" has yielded significant new construction, in addition to keeping a lot of older buildings occupied. Many nine-to-five commuters stay around to eat and drink and entertain themselves downtown as well; and several thousand have even decided to settle here. But they, like the other neighborhood folks, would not likely have shown up except for the general evacuation that the failure of Babbitt's city produced. You can only be a pioneer—urban or otherwise—if somebody provides you with a wilderness.

Thus, the "rediscovery" of downtown is not a rediscovery of anything. On the contrary, it is an invention based on the opportune exploitation of empty space, though the means of invention surely differ with regard to class. This space was not found; it had to be created by the sort of coverage that makes the absence of culture seem appealing, which is particularly true for the city's formerly chosen subjects. In that connection, the novel—which has long been the privileged vehicle of middle-class culture—is placed in an equivocal relation to its own history. Nobody writes novels about this (still largely middle-class) city any more, or if they do, the novels they write try to revoke the narrative contract on which the form, like the city, had traditionally been founded. That's what it means to cover the downtown scene. "The question is the story itself," Paul Auster writes in *City of Glass*, his brilliant rendering of cultural evacuation, "and whether or not it means something is not for the story to tell" (7). Auster's New York is the paradigmatic space of coverage—a space that becomes novelistic precisely because of its emptiness and because of the potential it holds out to his enigmatic protagonist for getting lost:

> New York was an inexhaustible space, a labyrinth of endless steps, and no matter how far he walked, no matter how well he came to know its neighborhoods and streets, it always left him with the feeling of being lost. Lost, not only in the city, but within himself as well. . . . On his best walks, he was able to feel that he was nowhere. . . . New York was the nowhere he had built around himself, and he realized that he had no intention of ever leaving it again. (8–9)

As the passage makes clear, this "lost" city is not nostalgic, which is important. Or if there is nostalgia here, it isn't for a return to a "readable" metropolis, which would precisely–and destructively–fill the aftercultural space that enables both the novel and the city imagined in it.

Not all reinhabitations are so existentially stark as Auster's turns out to be. On the contrary, for a certain part of the middle class–thirtysomething, affluent, usually childless–it's cool to be downtown, funky, an adventure. But unlike Zenith, this isn't a destination you arrive at by narrative means. The city that the middle class left and now, selectively, "rediscovers" is one locatable only by "alternative" agency: a thematized fantasy of hipness and conversion chic. These are the times after culture, *MetroTimes*, as the title of a local alternative "publication of news and the arts" would have it. This journalistic metrospace models the larger space of the city after culture, with the historic form of the newspaper being converted to alternative use. Appropriately, the "news" here is all about space: where to listen and watch, where to see and be seen. *Space* itself—as noun, as category—plays a crucial part in downtown discourse, as Fredric Jameson has noted (1984: 64): loft space, conversion space, artists' space, performance space, and so on.

The economy that governs this space is one of secrets rather than news, with the question being not how to shop, but how to stay covered: how to walk so you don't get mugged, how to get your fixture fee back from your landlord when you leave your loft, how to park, how to tip a doorman, how to get into an after-hours club, how to avoid talking to street people. How, in other words, to find and maintain the space of that invisible and desirable (and almost wholly individual) city that comes after culture. This alternative space is made desirable precisely because it is not generally known. Or at least this is the impression that coverage works to achieve. Thus there emerges the crucial problem of maintaining one's space, which lands the individual in a perpetual informational puzzle. "No matter how far he walked," Auster writes of his hero Quinn, "no matter how well he came to know its neighborhoods and streets, [the city] always left him with the feeling of being lost" (8). Unlike the teacherly city of middle-class reading, information here is not institutionalized but privately, even secretly, traded; this is why the city looks and feels the way it does. This is also why the novel can no longer be the first line of news writing (any more than a newspaper, even an alternative one, can).

With regard to the momentary economy of information, the always day-old medium of print becomes anachronistic, out of date. It can neither compensate nor cover the space that exists after culture. For that purpose, different forms are required, forms typified by television, in particular the TV news, which makes up for the secret that culture has become by appearing, informationally, to render everything knowable, and watchable, twenty-four hours a day. The sense of the word *coverage* we usually associate with news stories dates from the early nineteenth century. It seems first to have appeared in relation to betting and insurance: covering a loss. And that is still the point of coverage today; it covers the losses that its own operation depends on. In that connection, if the news were really what it claims to be—something new, and therefore outside conventional assumptions about the world—then its relevance would be minimal because most people live inside rather than outside convention. For that matter, the suspicion that middle-class conventions are no longer conventionally dependable makes for the current "fear of falling." News that really did what it claims would only advance such fears; it would be upsetting, then, rather than useful, like Orson Welles's infamous "War of the Worlds" broadcast, or like stories about radon in the basement or benzene in the Perrier. Too much information and the world becomes unlivable. Which means that the news—if it is to sustain a culture of whatever sort—must always be subverting the novelty on which it supposedly depends. And not only that, it must cover that subversion, or loss, if its own authority is to be maintained. In other words, the news is not so much about the world as it is about the ways people want and need to *feel* about the world and each other. This point is itself not news, obviously.

In this connection, television coverage does—in one sense—share a great deal in common with both newspapers and novels, which have historically provided the middle class with the news of the world—and especially the city—they needed in order to believe in their own entitlements. In his classic study of the novel, and its relation to the "rise" of middle-class culture, Ian Watt makes the (by now) familiar observation that the novel's

> primary criterion was truth to individual experience—individual experience which is always unique and therefore new. The novel is thus the logical literary vehicle of a culture which, in the last few centuries, has set an unprecedented value on originality, on the novel; and it is therefore well named. . . . What is often felt as the formlessness of the novel, as compared, say, with tragedy or the ode, probably follows from this: the poverty of the novel's formal conventions would seem to be the price it must pay for its realism. (13)

As Watt's comment suggests, and as middle-class critics seem never to tire of pointing out, the formlessness of the novel (no less than the class whose culture it records) is only apparent. And necessarily so. The news keeps on being new, necessarily, but it arrives in forms "always already" appropriate, and accountable, to the needs of the class for whom it is/was being reported. In particular, novelty must reciprocate the time-bound intelligence of story-telling through which middle-class individuals have historically understood and reproduced themselves ideologically.

The coverage that comes after culture must confront the no less pressing need of individuals to comprehend a world that has visibly outmoded traditional expectations about what time amounts to and how it is to be managed. In that sense, coverage differs significantly from the economy of representation that preceded it. For that matter, coverage stages, moment to moment, the exhaustion of representation: it introduces time-generated representations into a nonnarrative space only to demonstrate their informational inadequacy, their need for perpetual supplementation. Coverage, then, is always parasitic on representation. But this parasitism is itself always being covered—like the vampire's fangs—so that the evolution of news appears seamless, and that, as Watt said, "would seem to be the price it must pay for its realism."

Consider the production of the 11:00 p.m. report. Like the exposed, and usually brightly colored, pipes and conduits of any postmodern space, the utilities here are all out in the open for view. We are introduced to the final report by first being shown the set from which it will originate: cameras, cables, lights, lots of activity, the news-stars adjusting their microphones. Then the red light blinks on camera one, and the news begins. "Our lead story tonight," the head anchor might say, "is about a fire that gutted the historic Himelhoch Brothers Building downtown." What everyone watching has now been taught is that each element of this aleatory narrative enters an otherwise neutral space. We have already been shown that prior to the arrival of the news, there is nothing here but an empty set. But this innocence is illusory—an act of coverage, the point of which is to cover the humiliation of the precise materials on which the news ostensibly depends.

In the story about the fire next door, for example, there will be a number of different videotaped segments, together with live camera reports. In each case what happens is the same. A finally inconsequential event that most people understand well enough—a fire story—is first cut into very small pieces, each so small as to prohibit the fulfillment of the very narrative teleology on whose behalf this "story" is being told. Then pictures are displayed representing each segmented bit, but in every instance, the pictures are humiliated of any independent authority since their meaning is no longer self-evident. The viewer is never exposed to unmediated images. Instead, we usually see a picture of somebody else looking at a picture, or else watching something being pictured, and then (of necessity, it seems) telling us over and over that this is a fire—a fire that will not (because it is out) affect anyone now watching. The "reality" of news coverage, in other words, depends on the humiliation of narrative time along with the representations to which taped footage might appear to refer. Because both are now informationally inadequate, they must be supplemented by recursive and interruptive commentary. We can tell, then, when a story is really hot by the amount of layering that its coverage requires. Instacam footage with an on-site reporter narrating, intercut with eye-in-the-sky shots, ending—perhaps—with a split-screen dialogue of reporter and studio anchor doing a fast round of Q and A: that, and not some putative signified, is what makes for the reality of the news. If traditional narrative representation were what people sought, they'd sell their TV sets and buy lifetime subscriptions to the *New York Times.* That they don't attests to something more going on.

That something more one encounters not at a theoretical level, as an indictment of representation, but affectively, as the experience of being covered: the Super Bowl Effect, as it might be called. Why do millions of people watch the Super Bowl every year? Not, usually, because they are curious about how the game will end. In all but a few rare cases, the narrative outcome is a foregone conclusion. People watch, then, not so much to find out what will happen, but to see how the game is covered (and to be covered by it), and that—the coverage—takes on an independent reality of its own, which has to be participated in directly if you are to keep up with the news. For example, commenting on the falling audience share during the third and fourth quarters of the game, Michele Szynal, an ad executive for Gillette, said, "I don't think anyone's disappointed. It's still great to be associated with the Super Bowl, even with lousy numbers. We want to be in the Super Bowl because it's the premier event" (Markiewicz 1990: 7A). Here, it is not a matter of a televised representation of events displacing the real thing. Coverage *is* the real thing, the "premier event"; it defines the informational loop through which the news must circulate in order to *be* news. What you learn watching the Super Bowl—as opposed to the Thornton's fire my parents took me to when I was young—is how informationally impoverished the "real world" has become.

In that context, it is often (mistakenly) suggested that the news is merely an extension of the larger entertainment and advertising interests of TV, with the notion of "infotainment" having by now become a cliché. Nothing could be further from the truth, though. The news doesn't imitate the rest of TV; it's just the other way around: the whole of television becomes concurrent, progressively, with the coverage provided by the TV news. Thus the "menu-driven" aspect of popular network programs. Producers have merely adapted their structure from the news, which replaces plot with recurring segments. Narrative time is trivialized by its segmentation into various thematized bits, which are cued appropriately for viewer convenience, but which need not be assembled into any greater whole. As Rick Altman has argued, "Attention to American television narrative is mainly *menu-driven.* For the spectator firmly planted in front of the television, the menu is made clear by the images. For the half of the audience whose eyes are not glued to the tube, however, the sound track must serve to *label* the menu items" (45). Not only does the supposed teleology of narrative fulfillments dissolve (by popular demand), so too does the authority of visual representation as such because, as Altman points out, at least half the people "watching television" aren't even looking at the screen. But still they are *covered.* And that's the point.

Inasmuch as coverage is the purpose of TV, it takes precedence, which is why *Oprah* gets preempted by reports of an inconsequential apartment fire. Regular programming may be concurrent with coverage, sharing its informational agenda, but it can never take precedence over "live" events, and the opportunity they provide for reauthorizing the space of the news. The news, like the city, is always going on, so that from time to time special coverage must be allowed in to indemnify the informational authenticity of the medium. That is the difference between the periodic, and narratively closed, reporting of novels and newspapers and the open-endedness of TV. In this sense, then, the screen space is *always* the space of coverage, even when the set is off or when regular programs are on, because coverage is perpetually (potentially) in progress and might at any moment break in. And when it does, we see that the people who report the news are "always already" at work. The appeal of that "always already" gives rise to C-Span and other cable news services and keeps the rest of television "honest."

Coverage is not something external that happens *to* the middle class, therefore. Middle-class culture *is* the culture of coverage: each would be unimaginable without the other. "The practical problem of urban design now is how men and women can cope with the solitude imposed upon them by modernism," Sennett pointed out (1987: 7). But modernism is not the cause. Solitude has been the point; it has defined the necessary discipline (and ultimately the triumph) of middle-class individuality, all along, which has been obvious at least since George Babbitt drove off toward Zenith. Modernism, then, is merely one of the more powerful means toward an inevitable end. And now modernism has built a place for the individual to call home: the glass enclosed "nowhere" that Auster imagines at the end of our long narrative of arrival. And that—nowhere—is the space that now constitutes the prestige forms of middle-class coverage, just as it does the empty space—the space out of time—from which the news arrives.

Consider, for example, the inability of autochthonous cultures to resist the coverage that comes from nowhere. To what culture is the space (let alone the food) of MacDonald's or Wendy's or Arby's or Long John Silver's native? Yet where—now—has this "culture" from nowhere not displaced the mom-and-pop natives that preceded it? Or whose ethnicity do America's favorite ethnic spaces model: Chi-Chi's, Bennigan's, the Magic Pan, the Magic Wok? Or what about the clothes that America puts on when pursuing such favorite leisure activities as dining? From whose lives do the Sears and Penney and Spiegel collections derive? Not that some clothes—or foods—are more natural than others. They are all, equally, made up. Interesting here, however, is the near total collapse of local cultures when challenged by the culture from nowhere. Or there is tourism itself. It's often pointed out that when people are away from home, they want "no surprises," as Holiday Inn's ads used to say, so they stay in places—each one indistinguishable from the rest—none of which looks remotely like a home. So, what's the point?

The point is staying covered, and for that purpose, traditional, historic forms are usually not nearly so desirable as the culture that comes from nowhere.

Which is not to say that coverage is a process of simple alternatives: one thing instead of another. On the contrary, coverage, as I have pointed out, is a parasitic or viral relation. Once the host is exhausted, the apparatus of coverage is incapable of reproducing itself, which is why the thing being covered must always be preserved or else a replacement must be found. There is the case of urban renewal, for example. Despite the name, *renewal* has nothing to do with the making new of things that are old. Quite the contrary. My neighborhood is a successful "urban renewal" project with high property values and occupancy rates and low crime statistics. And perhaps most important of all, a good number of postsuburban middle-class returnees. But nothing here is being renewed. The "park" where I live, and the kinds of high rise structures built in it, are intended to preempt the evolved narrative culture for which the historical city stands: the small stores and shops, the cheap houses of "Black Bottom," which occupied the site now literally *covered* by my building. At the same time, however, the viral economy of renewal can be maintained only so long as the (apparently undesirable) city resists total exhaustion. If downtown were ever to achieve the bland sameness of a "good" suburb, then its investment potential would be at an end, along with the various abatements, kickbacks, and tax breaks that make renewals attractive, both financially and culturally. In that sense, the renewal will last only as long as it fails to achieve its ostensible goal.

By contrast, great numbers of people who live here undertake genuine renewals, which have nothing to do with coverage. In fact, coverage usually prohibits their renewal projects from continuing. In my city there are by some estimates as many as 60,000 homeless people. Particularly when the weather turns cold, they seek shelter in abandoned downtown buildings, of which there is a very large supply: old hotels, offices, department stores, banks, and so on, most of them relatively near the social service agencies that the homeless are forced to depend on. These structures are largely the concrete outcome of Babbitt's culture of narrative arrival. Just as downtown was the climax of the trip toward culture, each old building at the city's center is organized narratively as well; each works toward an analogous, architectural climax. These structures appear to gather strength from the (once) enviable real estate on which they stand and then gradually to climb up, and up, narrowing through progressive stories and setbacks toward the spires and flagpoles and observation decks from which a person (in the old days) could look down at a world that appeared all to converge on one special, climactic point. (It is a far different affair to drop into the city from nowhere, as I have, and to watch it as outsider, from an ungrounded isolation.) Those now abandoned places are genuinely renewed whenever they are taken over by the native residents of downtown. But as soon as such renewals get covered—by the news or other civic authorities—they are undone. As everyone knows, the unconverted past is, by law, proscribed, off limits, condemned.

My building, by contrast, has little in common with the old architecture of vertical progress. Along with the other high-rise structures in the park, it doesn't seem to have grown from the narratively charged earth at all, but to have fallen into it from above, from "nowhere," as Auster might say. Some of these glass-encased landing craft—particularly the ones by Mies—have not yet even touched down. They hover several feet above the ground on poured concrete colonnades, as if the alien surface were still too uncertain to be broached. Nevertheless, the historical forces that might once have kept us out, or up in the air, are now sufficiently weakened—humiliated—so that they can be turned to the viral ends of coverage. And just as the novel both told a story and also concealed the price one paid for belief, coverage too is a form of concealment. In that sense, then, it is possible to avoid being fooled simply by refusing to enter this space, just as one might have remained intentionally illiterate in a readerly world. While that response may bring with it certain satisfactions, it also means missing out on the news, which—like the real estate underneath my building—is still here, despite its being so desirably covered.

## V: Souvenirs

Just as the novel offered souvenirs of a culture based on time, coverage invites souvenirs of an afterculture organized by space. The novel produced the fantasy of temporal mastery, and the imaginary power that well-spent time would confer in the managing of significant objects: learning how to shop, in other words. Even for those who hadn't really learned how to shop, the novel brought anticipatory souvenirs (and enticements) of what it would feel like when they did. Novels are still being written, obviously, but the temporal mastery imagined by their narratives has become, as Auster says, more a question than an answer. In other words, novels are no longer capable of reporting the news about class and power—news that now has more to do with the *space* of info/serv than with the narrative *time* of production. Coverage, then—in its various aftercultural manifestations—brings souvenirs of the mastery of space, which (as with time previously) it is far easier to imagine controlling than it is to control in fact. In this way, coverage preserves the imaginary security of social class, often against significant, external challenge.

Consider the city once more. The class for whom it used to script the collective text of arrival now visit their "unreadable" town only selectively and most often through virtual means such as the evening news or televised sports broadcasts. When the return becomes actual, the nonresident middle class "come back" to spaces fully restored: the spaces after culture, from which the narrative debris of historical time has been removed, so that old things—warehouses, machine shops, lofts, cheap hotels—are made to look new again. But new in a way that they never looked even when they were. That is the difference between the time that was and the space that is. The newness that covers the past is all anachronistic, so that diners eat where lathe operators used to make auto parts; they drink and flirt and dance where beaver pelts used to get aged. The spaces now sought out as desirable destinations all humiliate the accumulated time that made them (prior to the coverage of "restoration") precisely what they had become: places to work. Now they—like much of the city in general—have been converted to a profitable, recreational emptiness.

Places that are merely old, and not yet restored, are generally to be avoided: in some cases, quite reasonably, because they are dangerous; but more often because unconverted space—space that was already here when people first decided to leave—is incapable of yielding souvenirs. There is, for example, the 411 lounge, which I've never heard anybody call by its name; only the address is used: "411." The place, and the people in it, look as if they've been here a long time. The pool table is in the back, pushed up too close against the far wall. If you need to make a shot from the corner, near the rail, you have to use one of the variably shortened cues, the smallest of which is the size of a drumstick and about eighteen inches long. That's how close to the wall the table is. Games cost a quarter, beer a dollar (premium brands, which means Heineken, are fifty cents extra). Things are cheap, but rarely friendly. Still, if you want a game, or a drink, you can get one, no questions asked. Even though this is among the oldest continuously operating saloons in downtown, and one of only two left where you can still play pool (after a fashion), not many people come here, least of all returnees. And that's not because the 411 is just "waiting to be discovered." Every big town has places like this: half empty, maybe, but still too full of the times—and people—that prevent their appealing to a touristic clientele. Which means that visits spent here yield no usable souvenirs. Even the regulars, I suspect, come to the 411 to forget rather than remember where they have been.

Better stick to the places where you can count on being fully covered. They, of course, are much easier to find and recall. Like the 11:00 report, they advertise their locations, specifically according to the conversion logic that comes after culture. Just around the corner from the 411, for example, there's Marilyn's on Monroe (a gay nineties/neon restoration bar with a cook who specializes in short orders) or there's Fishbone's Rhythm Kitchen (where a thematized version of New Orleans' past gets served up along with deracinated Cajun cuisine). In both instances, and in most successfully restored places downtown, the visuals are emphasized, with lots of neon and quotably thematized decor, all of which is made accessible by the plentiful application of plate glass. The windows here, unlike those in old, unrecovered places (even expensive ones), are meant to function as huge projection screens through which sociality is transacted. No matter which side of the glass you're on, you are inside the coverage that defines the reason for coming back to this newly constructed space; street scene or restaurant scene, that's still where you are: in a *scene*. Such visits based on seeing and being seen—whether actual or only by televisual proxy—risk little or nothing, which is the point.

So, while the history of the city is being visibly effaced, the effacement is being (often quite beautifully) covered, which anticipates the needs of the middle class generally, and not only those who return. Even for the people who are still resident, the historic life of the city is no longer shared, *in the body*, whether individual or collective. From my imaginary point, outside the glass of my co-op and outside my actual body, I understand the city by looking down at it from a private nowhere, just as visitors come back to a nowhere of images constructed in anticipation of their desire, privately, to return home. And we are, all of us, secured by the prophylaxis of our insights: the culture we've seen through can no longer touch us. Like all the best things downtown, the ground of public experience (and responsibility) is now made private because people are concerned about protecting themselves against interventions that have come to be historically associated with the city—interventions of criminality, disease, illiteracy. Although the results of this dissociation may be regrettable—the divorce of the body from the space of social communication—the motives behind it are understandable because the historical city—along with its schools, courts, agencies—is no longer capable of producing the information and service necessary to sustain the class that once lived here, the class that has subsequently had to find their livelihoods (no less than its security) elsewhere.

Middle-class individuals are now fixed by information. Information fixes their careers in the sense that it solves the question of what they are supposed to do. And it also fixes them in the sense that the individual becomes the—now—overdetermined site where multiple informational discourses converge and contest one another for control. *Life* gives way to life-*style*, and freed from any singular, narrative agenda, there's no reason styles can't change, day to day, even moment to moment. For that matter, sites can support overlapping addresses simultaneously; in fact, the "culture" encourages such overinterpretation. Just as the news has gotten over the univocal economy of narrative, the individual gets over the economy of "character" that would make the multiplication of personal addresses distressing rather than desirable, which is the "point" understood—syntactically, as *language*—by Barrett Watten's poem, "Direct Address":

> Address itself, to the world.
> Some kind of breakdown.
> A bird, almost inverted. The anarchy of production,
> rugs.
> Stripped, and the words are *there.*
> In computer-animated time. (57)

The end of the individual, like the end of the sentence (both telic and otherwise) is a final, informational fix, a turning inside out: the exposure of the language (of self) as dissociated elements, words that are "stripped," just *"there."* Like the trick played by plate glass in a high-rise building, when the body inside confronts a dematerialized image turned outside, our culture after culture manages the same inversion. But the loss—should anyone feel there to be one—is covered by the multiple convergence of effects.

The achievement of this inversion has been the destination of middle-class striving since the beginning. There is the central case of the department store, for example. The mastery of that commercial plot always lay at the top, in the furniture department. But once there, the individual—far from being "finished" or "complete"—was delivered into the hands of "interior decorators," whose command of domestic space—the "anarchy of production"—merely extended the dominion held by the store over its putative patrons. Given the limitations of the store, however, where people would live only intermittently, or in their fantasies, interiors could not be ideally exploited. Not so now: the public and private spaces of the culture have been conflated, so that the individual can be opened perpetually at multiple, inverted sites, to an informational management without the dissonance of outmoded, narrative "character."

The dissociation of narrative reference from the person referred to is paradigmatic of social class in general. On the one hand, class seems to have become elective, even trivial. It is no longer determining in a historical sense: the already written text that becomes your life, for good or ill. Forty years of inflation and easy credit have reduced the whole idea of traditional class roles to so much nonsense. At the same time, and perhaps not so happily, class (as a source of power and/or security) seems to have become a fearful conundrum the logic of which is hidden, or else accidental, precisely because it bears no fixed relation to real things. Objects, like individuals, no longer stand for a common cultural time invested in them, so that both take on a certain throw-away character. The logic of power relations appears secreted by the dissolution of a culture that turns out to have been only apparently their vehicle.

Classic, middle-class culture enfranchised objects as representing and presiding over a particular sort of time. And these objects, in turn, stood for the individual who was capable of owning and narrating their significance. The novel, then, tells the story of these desirable souvenirs; it teaches people how to quote their lives. The culture of info/serv is not quotable in the same way, however. Its forms are spatial rather than temporal. Souvenirs, like the whole discourse of quotation, are no longer possible in a classic, individual sense because the mechanism of quotation is all in the hands of others: media and service providers of every sort. Coverage, which defines the economy of souvenirs after culture, is not subject to narrative replay. Like the television news, or like conversion space generally, coverage is a matter of in/out, off/on. You're either covered or you're not, just as you're either in the informational circuit of the news or you're out of it. But once the set is off, once you leave the space of conversion, there's nothing to say or do or show to make real again—to memorialize—the value of what has gone on there.

Unlike the quotable objects that once stood for time and character, spatial references only mark—or "trace," as Derrida might say—the individual with the *absence* of cultural significance. For instance, you may prize your Hard Rock T-shirt as really having come from the (true) Hard Rock Cafe. Nevertheless, every time you put it on, you are saying more about where you are *not* than where, and who, you *are*.

The inverted subject of info/serv, who is also the subject of class after culture, is, therefore, at once both powerful and dependent: powerful because of the crucial ability to enter space, to turn the set on; but dependent because the same multiplication of addresses that constitutes coverage also dematerializes the individual who might stand for (or against) its colonization. This doubling of effects is perhaps best understood in the context of a club—a club such as often comes to occupy the converted space of an old downtown. One such establishment in my city, ClubLand, has taken over—reterritorialized—the space of the old Palms-State Theater, which is among the second-generation movie palaces built downtown in the 1920s. There, much as on a TV news set, the apparatus of coverage nightly humiliates the historic stage of representation into more relevant addresses. Crucially, the once centered and singular screen is replaced by three smaller screens that sit on top of a bank of TV monitors seventeen wide and three high. Each space is individually —informationally—addressable. Homologous with that spectacular transformation, the individual is also humiliated of singular, narrative competency. In the overdetermined space of ClubLand there is too much going on at any one moment to allow the concentration, the "focused attention," required to produce a traditionally conversational self. And that is what makes this a good place: the multiple stages and rooms, the volume, the lasers, the smoke machines. Each so floods the space with informational options as to render impossible the univocal narrative of self. Just try to explain to somebody who you are in there. You can't do it.

Not surprisingly, either, because the whole economy of time is here pointedly under attack. The communicated experience of duration—being bored, worrying that you've come on the wrong night, telling your friends you have to get up early in the morning—is a sign of weakness, a failure to be informed by the scene. Not by accident, then, the drug with class in this paradigmatic atmosphere was and is cocaine. Even for those who don't use cocaine (and they are probably the majority), its high covers the experience of what is supposed to happen here. Cocaine dissolves the claims that time, in the guise of fatigue, might otherwise urge against the body; it translates dependency into a delusion of competence and power; it makes the people of the moment seem like old friends. Under its sign, informational conversion is fully accomplished as narrative time gives way to a non-narratable economy of consumption without accumulation. The character who gets enough is—here—the one nobody wants to be with.

Admittedly, most middle-class people will never go to ClubLand, although for those who pretend to have mastered the informational return to the city of coverage, it is necessary, at least, to talk as if they have been there (and not merely as anthropologists). For all the rest, though, the power of ClubLand is no less present and far-reaching. The moves that it makes against the individual—the collapse of private with public space, the informational inversion of the body—are continuous with the news generally. In fact, the space of the news is defined by the same overdetermined convergence of addresses that achieves momentary climaxes at ClubLand or else in the commercials that sponsor the news. There the medium recites, in highly energized form, what the "program" has all along been teaching. And the lesson has been so effectively mastered that the necessary period of recitation grows shorter, rather than longer, with individual commercials declining in length from a minute to thirty seconds, to fifteen, and now to even shorter spans, so that moment to moment the subject of coverage is addressable by more and more bits of highly energized information. And no less than the info/serv body, upon which time is no longer supposed, biologically, to write, the space of coverage—because it is likewise "empty"—is not visibly altered by the passage through it of multiple, contradictory addresses. On the contrary, that is what it is here for and why it *is* empty.

But in this space outside time—whether personal or social—the memory of culture endures, and inevitably so for the class whose only tangible experience of power is founded on that same narrative individual who is now covered by informational disintegration. Thus the conflicted desire both to have a past and to erase it. Thus too, the apparently self-defeating nostalgia for souvenirs, which are available—ultimately—only in the past. Sameness cannot render intelligible, or quotable, the power of class; only difference seems worth recollecting (or being afraid of), precisely because it is different, because it marks a border between now and then, between here and there, inside and out, us and them. But for the inverted individual, no less than the inverted city—the city reimagined from *nowhere*—borders are discoverable only in the past. In the here and now, the city is unreadable; whatever differences it may actually contain are reduced to a uniform coverage.

The insufficiency of the present and the viral economy of coverage lead to the Taco Bell Phenomenon, which is a nostalgic response to the otherwise unquotable space that defines class after culture. In a series of stylish commercials advertising the food chain, one or more adventuresome (and presumably hungry) white people "make a run for the border," which is marked only by the fulfillment of their desire to find a franchise restaurant specializing in retro-food: *retro* in the sense that a deracinated past—or pastness—is being used to cover the lost authenticity of the present: the pastness of the old world, of the American southwest, of colonial/gringo nostalgia generally. And as the commercials proudly boast, they've already "got your order" even before you begin your run for their/our border, so that "we" need never confront any "others" at the border; we only find more people like ourselves, who have grown nostalgic for difference, but prefer to avoid its native signified.

The nightly return of the news, like the return visits of suburban residents to downtown, is founded on this paradigmatic Taco border. The old, historically inscribed differences of the city—differences of race and class and political entitlement—are obscured, with the loss of history being covered by the self-authorizing comprehension of the news. And the precise experience of being in the space where the covering gets done makes this "culture" desirable. So you go to ClubLand because it is both new and old; you go there simultaneously to remember where you are and also to forget it, just as you go with friends because of who you are but also to lose track of who you are. You other yourself by going back in time to (what is now) *their* city, eating *their* food, converting *their* buildings, but you cover the otherness and whatever threats it might pose by playing it out on your own plate glass screens, which provide both insight and also separation. You always watch the news expecting something different, but knowing all the while that the news is good precisely insofar as it *makes* no difference. And all these things you choose to do, though there seems little choice about the choosing because at this border your order has already been taken, even before it was placed.

As such, coverage becomes preoccupied with the city, no less so than the audience on whose behalf coverage is undertaken because the city now—perhaps more than at any time in its past—still acts for the differences that are elsewhere obscured, covered over. Here, evacuations both actual and ideological have left the skeletal remains of difference closer to the surface: poverty and plenty cohabit, people elsewhere invisible (addicts, mental patients, prostitutes, the poor, the sick, the homeless) find homes. That aspect of the city makes it appear not only more threatening but also more real because it is made up of the same contested but covered borders that still figure our nostalgias for legible class and power. Knowledge of each, however, is obscured by coverage. At the same time, only as coverage can the social and political reality of those borders be grasped in the context of actual power relations.

But the fact of coverage need not cancel the good that a creative nostalgia might do; and that—nostalgia—may be the only role left at this point for the faculties we used to refer to collectively as *memory*. "The language of critique is effective," Homi Bhabha has written, "to the extent to which it overcomes the given grounds of opposition and opens up a space of 'translation': a place of hybridity, figuratively speaking, where the construction of a political object that is new, *neither the one nor the Other*, properly alienates our political expectations" (10–11). Or there is this by Guillermo Gómez-Peña: "The border is not an abyss that will have to save us from threatening otherness, but a place where the so-called otherness yields, becomes us, and therefore [becomes] comprehensible." Thus nostalgia leads people, after long rides, through wild regions, to feel the desire for a city, as Calvino understood, even a failed city like mine; thus too, perhaps, the possibility exists for constructing in the space of coverage, which is also the space of political understanding, an object beyond our nostalgias: one "that is new, *neither the one nor the Other*."

# Shopping

## The Decay of Modernism and the Difficult Life of Objects after Culture

*The exposed, outer life of the city cannot be simply a reflection of inner life. Exposure occurs in crowds and among strangers. The cultural problem of the modern city is how to make this impersonal milieu speak, how to relieve its current blandness, its neutrality, whose origin can be traced back to the belief that the outside world of things is unreal. Our urban problem is how to revive the reality of the outside as a dimension of human experience.*

—Richard Sennett, *The Conscience of the Eye*

### I: Gatsby's Smile

When Nick Carraway glanced up into Jay Gatsby's brilliant smile, one evening in an imaginary West Egg, Long Island, in the summer of 1922, the crisis on which Modernism is founded at once became clear, and personal. "He smiled understandingly," Nick recalls:

> It was one of those rare smiles with a quality of eternal reassurance in it, that you may come across four or five times in life. It faced—or seemed to face—the whole external world for an instant, and then concentrated on *you* with an irresistible prejudice in your favor. It understood you just as far as you wanted to be understood, believed in you as you would like to believe in yourself, and assured you that it had precisely the impression of you that, at your best, you hoped to convey. (48)

Under the gaze of that uncanny smile, Nick does more than complete the little joke of his surname, momentarily casting his *cares away*; he arrives at a whole new understanding of what the past has meant and what it will (and will not) mean to him in the future. Or at least he feels for a time as if he might have approached such a utopian consummation. But just at the moment when the imaginary "best" seems about to incarnate itself, "precisely at that point [the smile] vanished" (48). The inventedness of Gatsby's smile—like the inventedness of Modernism itself—threatens at every moment to emerge and overwhelm this desirable confidence game with the truth of arbitrary fabrication because that—fabrication—is both the source of its power and the cause of its undoing. "Precisely at that point [the smile] vanished," Nick recalls, "and I was looking at an elegant young roughneck, a year or two over thirty, whose elaborate formality of speech just missed being absurd" (48). The subject, then, is not Gatsby so much as it is Nick, or rather the desire that Nick is allowed to play out on the larger-than-life screen of Gatsby's smile.

Fitzgerald's lyrical (if conflicted) meditation was neither a popular nor a critical success in 1925, when *The Great Gatsby* first appeared; his earlier, less ambiguously freighted works, fared better with contemporaries. For the majority of Americans, it would take several generations and another world war to make the inflationary ambiguity of Nick's situation representative. And by then, the novelty of Gatsby's smile would have become commonplace, a matter of advertising cliché and self-help pap, so that the crisis brought on by first apprehension would give way—eventually—to the disinterested *attitude* that defines the present, *post*modern moment. Which is not to say that the crisis of Fitzgerald's novel is any less real now than it was sixty-odd years ago; only that crisis itself has become a predominating, and to some extent even a consoling, figure of contemporary coverage. We grow so accustomed to the effect of Gatsby's self-authorizing smile, endlessly—commercially—inflated, that Nick's crisis seems likewise romantic in its outdatedness.

In this context, the outmoded city—perhaps more than any other element of our representational culture—stands for the material postlife of high Modernism. "Ward off anguish by absorbing its causes," or so goes the evangelical dictum of Le Corbusier (Tafuri 131). That America's cities have failed, by popular agreement, that they will first have to "come back" if they are still meaningfully to exist at all, has not meant an end to the dispensation according to which Modernism represented their utopian potential, however. "Ward off anguish by absorbing its causes": that's still what cities are doing, except their millenarianism is now "inverted," as Fredric Jameson has pointed out (1984: 53). In this sense, then, the city stands for the crisis of representational culture generally. Or rather, it stands for the exhaustion of that crisis and the loss of the perfectible potential inherent in Gatsby's smile. On the one hand, the city remains a powerful, representative force. Above all, it preserves—regardless of how haphazardly—the millenarian moment of high Modernism; the institutions of civic culture were born of the hope that past ills would here submit to enlightened, bureaucratic rationalization. On the other hand, and at the same time, the city stands for the failure of those same institutions to realize their utopian promise. It's the place where things go, or get sent, to go wrong, particularly as they become subject to institutional care. Which in no way diminishes the representational power of the city, or its usefulness. Just the reverse: precisely because the city is still so powerfully representative (albeit in inverted form), it can become the dumping ground—both actual and figurative—for everything the middle class must leave behind if it is to preserve its utopian franchise, in ever more highly individualized (and *sub*urbanized) forms.

What has been lost in the progressive familiarity of Gatsby's smile, and the crisis it invites, then, is the potential of that cultural surface to become a terrain of what de Certeau calls the practice of "strategy" and "tactics," borrowing his terms from Clausewitz. "In our societies," he says

> as local stabilities break down, it is as if, no longer fixed by a circumscribed community, tactics wander out of orbit, making consumers into immigrants in a system too vast to be their own, too tightly woven for them to escape from it. But these tactics introduce a Brownian movement into the system. They also show the extent

> to which intelligence is inseparable from the everyday struggles and pleasures that it articulates. Strategies, in contrast, conceal beneath objective calculations their connection with the power that sustains them from within the stronghold of its own "proper" place or institution. (xx)

Our present, informational inflation has robbed Gatsby's smile of its uncanny potential; it has so domesticated the crisis of representation—the immediate confrontation of seeing and believing—as to obscure the *tactics* actually (and also potentially) in use, which leads de Certeau to the conclusion that we need a "politics" of "everyday practice" (xxiv). Such a politics might seem a simple enough matter on Gatsby's imaginary lawn; it remains to be seen whether that politics is possible in the real space of present cultural representations.

## II: Inside the Representing Engine

There is an extraordinary sequence in David Cronenberg's film *Videodrome* (1983). The main character, played by James Woods, begins a particularly intense affair with a woman portrayed by the faded pop star, Deborah Harry. Through various elements, both thematic and physical, the basis of the affair is developed as an urge on both characters' parts to *get at* each other. Pornographic videos give way to straight sex, which in turn gives way to sadomasochism. But still the two haven't really gotten what they need. At that point, a sci-fi plot device allows Debbie Harry to enter the TV and become a representation herself, on the same screen where she and the Woods character have lately been watching a snuff film. And from inside the set she calls back to him, which is when Cronenberg achieves a truly brilliant effect. As Harry approaches the screen surface from the other (in)side, the set is anthropomorphosed; she beckons to Woods, who approaches, as she does, the screen membrane between them becoming filled with a now pulsating representation of her lips. Woods comes close, right up to the set, and then he inserts himself into her/its mouth, only to emerge, subsequently, on the other side in the informational domain of images. Finally, he gets at her—*really*—by entering through her, through the appropriated female body of desire, the representing engine of television. Once there, of course, he is neither more nor less "real" than any other image, which is the point.

The brilliance of this sequence consists in its figuring in a particularly arresting way the crisis that overtakes a representational culture in which the representing agents are no longer directly accessible. The city—along with its various institutions—may still stand for culture, but it no longer offers a way in (any more than a real TV set). Its routes of access are all blocked: either they are abandoned, or else they become the objects of recreational conversion (and trivialization). Whatever kinds of knowing the city stands for, then, it will not be of help to individuals who live in a material world that they no longer produce. The city, in other words, is no longer about "the practice of everyday life," as de Certeau calls it. At least not for the middle class. On the contrary, the city merely concretizes the alienation of info/serv managers and workers from a world of someone else's production. Like Gatsby's suddenly historicized lawn, it is "material without being real," in terms of the work people do (now) and the things they know. Nevertheless, the fact remains that the material body of the culture is one that we necessarily inhabit and consume; otherwise life would not be possible. But it is a body no longer real to us, no longer expressive of our history, except as the pseudo-history of our desires to possess the objects of some still industrial Other. Thus Cronenberg's brilliant figuration of desire, which locates the body—under information—as the most interesting object of all, but not until it, like Debbie Harry, has been seen through.

Gatsby's smile problematizes the relation between a represented "real" and a "material" given: the gesture remains crucially distinct from the objects that it nominally stands for. By contrast, Cronenberg's film problematizes the loss of the material world as a referential fix on what is real, and specifically in terms of the public, informational space of television. The Woods character realizes his most intimate private fantasies by dissolving himself—no less than the objects of his desiring—into the two-dimensional publicity of television. He completes the trip that Gatsby only, imperfectly, began.

Commenting on this loss of distinctions, Jean Baudrillard has maintained that both public and private, material and real, dissolve simultaneously into "obscenity," which makes all the more difficult the already complex life of objects no less than individuals:

> In a subtle way, this loss of public space occurs contemporaneously with the loss of private space. . . . Their distinctive opposition, the clear difference of an exterior and an interior exactly described the domestic *scene* of objects. . . . Now this opposition is effaced in a sort of *obscenity* where the most intimate processes of our life become the virtual feeding ground of the media. . . . Inversely, the entire universe comes to unfold arbitrarily on your domestic screen (. . . like a microscopic pornography of the universe, useless, excessive, just like the sexual close-up in a porno film). . . . Obscenity begins precisely . . . when all becomes transparence and immediate visibility, when everything is exposed to the harsh and inexorable light of information and communication. (130)

Or to cast this in the more market driven (and romantic) discourse of futurology, "We are drowning in information but starved for knowledge," as John Naisbitt put it in his multimillion-selling popularization *Megatrends* (1984: 17).

That the loss described here is real rather than rhetorical is at once obvious in the city and particularly for the objects—and bodies—that the city once so desirably contained, but which it is no longer capable of comprehending or defending. The (now) historically humiliated city has proved incapable of preserving its contents in suitably opaque forms. That, more than anything else, is what occasions the moment of postmodern insight, whether that moment is perceived as an inversion or a radical break; and it also makes possible the "obscene" vandalism that overwhelms urban space and the people trapped in it.

The invested time of culture used to make things appear solid and powerful in the city, with the department store being virtually indistinguishable from the museum (or the bank) inasmuch as each institution memorialized (and mystified) the cumulative objectification of time. There lovable objects stood for what time had meant, or else might mean if properly invested, whether in the getting of culture or the getting of its products, which was the same thing. Imagining Carrie's first experience of a department store and the consumers inside it, Theodore Dreiser, for example, represents both in the following way:

> [Carrie] noticed too, with a touch at the heart, the fine ladies who elbowed and ignored her, brushing past in utter disregard of her presence, themselves eagerly enlisted in the materials which the store contained. . . . A flame of envy lighted in her heart. She realized in a dim way how much the city held—wealth, fashion, ease—every adornment for women, and she longed for dress and beauty with a whole heart. (26–27)

It is not that cities no longer contain stores with expensive objects or customers who would elbow a person not finely dressed. The difference is that cities—through the publicity of their institutions, commercial and otherwise—no longer write the romance of the objects or the people who consume them. Watch any given episode of *Lifestyles of the Rich and Famous*, for instance, and what you'll see is people *away* from town, people in a world of privately held and loved objects the mystery of which is preserved specifically by their celebrity: by their sequestration inside TV, in other words. And that is a far different affair from the romantic, and public, opacity institutionalized by the great stores and museums.

The city now, no less than its institutions, gives in to "obscenity," to use Baudrillard's term; it becomes a pornopticon wherein objects and bodies alike are deprived of their opacity, of the right to withhold an inside (however mystified) that differs from the visible outside: "Obscenity begins precisely . . . when all becomes transparence and immediate visibility, when everything is exposed to the harsh and inexorable light of information and communication" (Baudrillard 130). After culture, the city defines a space where everything can be seen, but where little remains real. It's where people come to engage the body. As it happens, the obscenity laws in most cities—as compared with the suburbs—are written specifically to elicit the transparency of local objects. They legislate the seeing through that defines desire after culture: seeing through clothes or the proprieties that might prohibit a person's understanding the display of "totally nude" bodies as entertainment; seeing through the statutes (whether formally or informally) that in other places would prohibit the sale of "obscene" books and pictures and services; seeing through the opacity of individual character so that one's own body becomes communicable here, if not entirely intelligible. "Ward off anguish by absorbing its causes": more and more, cities become the places where everyone gets to act like postmodern conventioneers, places so *obscene* that whatever goes on here doesn't have to be taken as real because nothing will ever come of it.

But events—no less than the objects and people that precipitate them—*are* real, of course. And no amount of seeming, regardless of how well intentioned, can erase that fact. Consider Baby Jessica, for example; or rather consider the comparison her televised representation offers. (She's the little girl who fell down a well in Texas and then got rescued, whose ordeal became the stuff first of live-action coverage, then of magazine accounts, then books, then made-for-TV movies, and finally—inevitably—of court battles.) It is true of most cities, and surely true of the one where I live, that every day lots of unknown Jessicas fall into one or another urban well: AIDS, prenatal crack or heroin addiction, malnutrition, neglect, abuse, or simply (if there can be such a thing) the effects of long-term poverty. Just like the well little Jessica fell down, these cultural fissures could be stopped so that no baby need ever disappear into them. That they are not, and that nobody seems particularly concerned over the hundreds of individuals daily dropping out of sight, says a great deal about how accustomed we have grown to the obscenity of our crisis and to the predicament of bodies that are now familiarly "material without being real." The little girl from TV compels great outpourings of feeling and action because her plight is an unfolding *news* story; the real children near at hand are rarely if ever attended to. And in some sense, this is inevitable because in terms of representation, and particularly in terms of what they, *in the city*, represent, what is there to *say*, or *see*, about them that is not always already known and therefore of no consequence?

Not only just children, obviously, become the "beneficiaries" of the city's inverted millennium. The same goes for great numbers of adults as well who are stuck with the "transparent" afterlife of urban objects and subjects. The city itself, for that matter, is no less liable to being seen through. All the empty informational space of graphs and charts represents what used to be here (people, dollars, cars, households, and on and on) and what is not here any more. And this translates into a physical transparency as well: empty lofts, abandoned houses, neighborhoods where no neighbors any longer obscure the view. There are derelict properties, and lives, of every sort that nobody wants to own up to, or support, and that "the city" sooner or later is forced to absorb institutionally, first through defaults and then, eventually, by demolition. "The debris of [Detroit's] vibrant past," wrote a staffer for the *Los Angeles Times*, "—vacant, burned-out homes, decaying, abandoned buildings, long-empty factories—is being bulldozed away under a massive city demolition and land clearance program designed to deal with a free-fall plunge in population" (Risen A14). The ironic point of the newspaper story is to record an amazing and probably unique fact about this city after culture. In a certain, obscene way, it is being returned to nature: "In the tall weeds among the thousands of abandoned buildings and vacant lots in this city, along vast corridors of once-bustling streets—now reduced to urban wilderness—pheasants from the rural brush are flourishing" (A14). In what has become characteristic fashion, the reporter's irony is founded on the still more ironic (if unself-conscious) assumption that a city so overfilled with human misery can be written about as if it were empty.

But to the reporter's credit, this is quite true in an informational sense. The representations that he imagines to define a city—streets, houses, civic buildings, great stores—now go uncaptioned by the desire of the citizens. The unshopped-in stores, the unlived-in houses, and the untenanted office buildings stand for the absence of any human accounting for what is here. So the pheasants make a better story than the million abandoned citizens who are still in Detroit, or at least one that is easier to tell. At the same time, it's not as if the residents haven't noticed the need somehow to label this seen-through place. Even in towns that are more traditionally prosperous, which is most of them, the withdrawal of middle-class culture from its once-favored sites has invited the genius of native caption writers. Starting with the basic "Fuck" message, the city seems to lend itself to being written on, particularly the parts that abandonment has rendered the most transparent, as one obscenity calls to another.

It is not just for the sake of obscenity that the writing goes on, however, perhaps not even primarily so. The available spaces of the city apparently need to be written on (as opposed to about) if they are to become intelligible, most of all for the people who still live here. So, esoteric captions of every sort appear on walls, windows, doors, buses, subway trains, people's bodies—anything that needs explaining. Each message might be construed as a *tactical* text, after de Certeau, a text explaining the meaning that abandoned things still have for anyone who understands what has become of them. Though not necessarily speaking of graffiti, he has argued that "these ways of reappropriating the product-system, ways created by consumers, have as their goal a *therapeutics for deteriorating social relations* and make use of techniques of re-employment in which we can recognize the procedures of everyday practices" (xxiv). Perhaps the most interesting use in my city of such a "therapeutics" came in a project by local artists who attached to abandoned downtown buildings photographic blow-ups of these same structures, or sometimes of their collapsed interiors. Each black-and-white representation, about three feet by five feet, carried the caption "Demolished By Neglect." What the project demonstrated, or rather what was demonstrated by reactions to it, is the "strategic" resistance of the authorities to any tactical appropriation of their captioning privileges. Graffiti, handbills, advertisements of every kind proliferate on each of the still abandoned structures addressed by the "demolished by neglect" project. Those signs don't seem to cause any problems whereas the others were immediately removed and attempts were made to prosecute the artists for vandalism. The difference, perhaps, is that in the latter instance, the crisis of representation and the question of who controls it, were unmistakably and self-consciously called into question.

As to why this should be so, and why the strategy of power is so intimately involved, Roland Barthes describes the following relation, not in the context of urban renewal, but with regard to the way that images and captions, or texts, interact:

> In other words, and this is an important historical reversal, the image no longer *illustrates* the words; it is now the words which, structurally, are parasitic on the image. The reversal is at a cost: in the traditional modes of illustration the image functioned as an episodic return to denotation from a principal message (the text) which was experienced as connoted since, precisely, it needed an illustration; in the relationship that now holds, it is not the image which comes to elucidate or "realize" the text, but the latter which comes to sublimate, patheticize or rationalize the image. (1977: 25)

Aside from making their point that a profitable neglect has demolished the city, the artists—in a more subtle way—have parodied the politics of image production by means of which civic representations are controlled. In the first instance, they point out that neglect (doing nothing) is, in fact, an act of production; as far as postmodern Detroit is concerned, it is *the* act of production responsible for the city's present state. For instance, virtually no part of the abandoned downtown is not owned. Its uninhabited spaces are bought and sold frequently, and at a profit, by people whose intention is to do nothing with them except to take advantage of the opportunities afforded by institutionally sanctioned neglect in terms of tax write-offs, bankruptcy defaults, resale of architectural details and fittings, and so on.

In the second, more subtle instance, the "Demolished" artists have tactically parodied the strategy that sustains the civic, representational apparatus and its power over urban space. "Formerly," Barthes maintains, "the image illustrated the text (made it clearer)." But now this relation has been reversed. "Today," Barthes says, "the text loads the image, burdening it with a culture, a moral, an imagination" (1977: 26), which is what he means by the "parasitic" relation that now obtains. Text becomes parasitic on image; the one derives sustenance from the slow decay of the other. And that is the point the "Demolished" artists are making: the point that institutional "captions" are parasitic on the very thing—the "city"—that they nominally interpret. Just as text connotatively infiltrates the photographic illustration, thereby naturalizing its own cultural operations, the civic discursive apparatus excuses a politics of neglect by its existence *here*, as the bureaucratic caption on this powerfully denotative place: "The closer the text to the image, the less it seems to connote it; caught as it were in the iconographic message, the verbal message seems to share in its objectivity, the connotation of language is 'innocented' through the photograph's denotation" (26). So too the political structure that runs this place is "innocented" by its very closeness to the illustrative demolition it depends on and benefits from. If this weren't Detroit, in other words, then none of this could be tolerated. The unstated corollary is that because this is Detroit, none of it finally matters.

Objects that exist in the city, whether human or otherwise, are no longer defended by a cultural enfranchisement; they become transparent, unreal in their "obscenity." For example, a couple of years before J. L. Hudson's closed their flagship store downtown, I went there to buy a bottle of ink. In the stationery department there were fountain pens on display costing up to several hundred dollars, but there was no ink for sale. No one was expected to treat that exotic merchandise as if it were still for actual use. Similarly, but in a much more sinister way, bodies—now undefended by culture—become no less unreal than objects. That is why so many miseries can be visited upon the bodies left here, undefended. And it is why violence becomes so predictable a part of city life, and not just in this city. When asked why he had attacked the anonymous woman who has come to be known as the "Central Park jogger," Yusef Salaam (age 15) told detectives, "It was something to do. It was fun" (Stone 35). The brutalizing of that woman is beyond excusing. But there is also the terrible failure of her attackers to recognize, in her body, any reality to which they might be held responsible, whether legally or morally. In that failure of recognition, they perhaps acted—and spoke—out of the cultural transparency that overtakes the city.

Nick Carraway imagines Gatsby's body talking to him, after Daisy has taken away his dream and Wilson has taken his life. "Look here, old sport," Nick imagines the body saying, "you've got to get somebody for me. You've got to try hard. I can't go through this alone" (166). Try as he will, Nick fails in that mission. Gatsby's undefended body can summon up neither desire nor compassion. One wonders if the city with all its bodies will fare any better.

## III: Mr. Spinks

Every suit I owned up until the age of ten I bought from Mr. Spinks, who worked in the men's department at Thornton's great downtown store in the small city where I grew up. Mr. Spinks was a slight, courtly man in whose judgment my mother—who was the one actually buying the suits—placed implicit and unquestioning faith. At the time when I first knew him, Mr. Spinks was probably in his late sixties; he retired while I was still in grade school, not long after Thornton's original store burned and my family abandoned the city for suburbia. He, of course, always had on a suit himself: jacket, pants and vest; navy blue with chalk stripes. His shoes were black, cap-toe oxfords; his glasses, rimless spectacles, of the sort that Sinclair Lewis imagined for George Babbitt, who would have been perhaps ten years older than Mr. Spinks. Across his vest, he wore a watch chain adorned with what I would, much later, come to recognize was a Phi Beta Kappa key. Mr. Spinks fixed in my boy's imagination—apparently without the least conscious effort on his part—an image that defined for years my notion of style.

After the slight bow that always opened our interviews, he would ask what I, which is to say my mother, was interested in. Then he would start talking about colors and fabrics and cut without making the slightest move to pick anything up. The clothes, like Barthes's classic newspaper photographs, were secondary to this exposition; pants and jackets merely served to illustrate his cultivated inquiry, which was the real concern. From his pedagogical captioning of the store's contents, I learned to respect (and be intimidated by) the profound opacity of things. I might wear the clothes he sold my mother, but I suspected I'd never be able to inhabit them with his proprietary insight. When I'd stand, looking in the mirror during a fitting, listening to him describe what I had on, feeling his fingers running behind a lapel, or making chalk marks on the back of my jacket, I'd try to remember everything he said. Then at home, alone, I'd try to caption my own private display with his recollected words so that I might live up to the illustrative clothes he had so meticulously fitted for me—clothes which had now taken on their own independent, denotative life.

Which returns things to the vexed ambiguity of Gatsby's smile. Or rather to the world enfranchised by his enigmatic gesture. Nick Carraway may have followed Fitzgerald inescapably back into the past and into the life that his "people" had for generations known there, but that was not the direction taken by *my* people, or by the middle class as a whole. By the time Mr. Spinks retired, we were headed elsewhere:

> Between 1950 and 1970, the suburban population doubled from 36 to 74 million, and 83 percent of the nation's total growth took place in the suburbs. In 1970, for the first time in the history of the world, a nation-state [America] counted more suburbanites than city dwellers or farmers. Perhaps the most remarkable statistic of all is . . . that of the fifteen largest metropolitan areas in the United States in 1980, only in Houston did a majority of residents [54.9%] live in the central city. (Jackson 283–84)

It wasn't only in a physical sense that people left the city and the past that the city represented, however. Just as they had abandoned the geographic space of the great towns, they abandoned the economy of centralized dreaming (and spending) represented by its business and cultural institutions. Mr. Spinks, like the store where he spent his career, simply got left behind: anachronistic relics both.

"We shall solve the city problem by leaving the city," as Henry Ford speculated in one of his more prophetic moments (Melder 469-71). And that is precisely what has happened.

The American middle class were no less tempted than Scott Fitzgerald by a contemplation of the "fresh green breast" of a new world —a world that lay beyond the city and beyond the historical burdens imposed by the past. The only difference is that the crisis he imagined led people not backward (as he had expected) but forward, toward the fulfillment of a house and a lawn and a car for every family. This is precisely where observers of the American scene so frequently get things wrong, and in precisely the way that Scott Fitzgerald imagined the cliché flimsiness of Gatsby's self-invention to be dangerous and self-revealing. Probably the most famous of such critics is Lewis Mumford. "In the mass movement into suburban areas a new kind of community was produced," he wrote in *The City in History* (1961):

> [A community] which caricatured both the historic city and the archetypal suburban refuge: a multitude of uniform, unidentifiable houses, lined up inflexibly, at uniform distances, on uniform roads, in a treeless communal waste, inhabited by people of the same class, the same income, the same age group, witnessing the same television performances, eating the same tasteless pre-fabricated foods, from the same freezers, conforming in every outward and inward respect to a common mold. . . . Thus, the ultimate effect of the suburban escape in our own time is, ironically, a low-grade uniform environment from which escape is impossible. (486)

But the fact remains that the uniform sameness of this projection renders the popular fulfillment of our modernist utopia both achievable and also desirable. A standardized, "uniform" architecture is both easier (and cheaper) to put up and to put up with.

And as the architect Robert Venturi has argued, "Many people like suburbia. This is the compelling reason for learning from Levittown" (154), with Levittown, of course, being surely the most famous—or perhaps infamous—example of Mumford's dreaded sameness and uniformity. He is surely not alone in his criticisms.

As Nicholas Lemann has pointed out, "American intellectuals since about the time of the First World War have been trying to prove that middle-class life is empty, while most Americans have enthusiastically embraced it" (46). Even so, Lemann concedes (referring to such classic works as *The Organization Man*) that "still, the dark side of suburbia was detected by so many observers that it's hard to believe they all just projected it from their own minds onto their subject matter" (46). In that context, he makes it a point to distinguish the first generation of postwar suburbia, which attracted so much negative commentary, from its subsequent, ex-urban continuation: throughout the initial moment of outward mobility, the central city retained a powerful role in the lives of commuters; by the arrival of the second moment, the city had become largely superfluous. And along with it, so too had the anxieties that animated the figural representation of Levittown: "Today nobody worries about conformity as a national issue, and nobody I met [in the suburbs] mentioned it as a problem. The suburban psychological force that occasionally overwhelms people is not the need to fit in but the need to be a success" (36). Which would lead to the conclusion that even at their weakest, the residents of Levittown were tactically more adept than the alarmist projections of strategic routinization would have inclined most observers to expect.

"Learning from Levittown," in other words, no less than its ex-urban progeny, involves more than establishing some (by now) rather simple oppositions: sameness versus diversity, conformity versus freedom, suburban tastelessness versus urban sophistication, bad versus good. It seems likely that even at its worst, the uniformity that commercial modernism wrought was not only, or perhaps even primarily, felt as a defeat. The affordable similitude of suburbia is also liberating. It means an end to, and seeing through of, the historic discipline and distinctions of culture. The inflationary plenty and easy credit that lay beyond the town (and beyond the Second World War) made it seem, at least, that democracy was achievable and that people, individually, could all finally escape the past to make a better life of their own. Today, it is arguable whether that optimistic projection has survived the economic fall-out of the

1980s. Nevertheless, the suburban lawn of Gatsby's dreaming is still where the majority of the middle class imagine their desires will be fulfilled (Jackson 4). People escape from the exclusionary restrictions of history by means of a congenial, inflationary entitlement. The gain is one of tactical opportunity, particularly for traditionally disenfranchised individuals; the loss is an isolation that comes after culture, when the once communicable idiom of history falls into neglect and finally dies.

The consequently ambiguous relation of individuals to the objects of their desire is perhaps nowhere clearer, and more clearly related to the green world of suburbia, than at the mall. Just as the department store stood for the city and reproduced it ideologically, the mall fulfills the same function for the suburbs. The point of the mall (any *good* one that is) is to contain people so successfully that it never occurs to anyone to make up a need different from the range of possibilities already anticipated there. It's easy to stay inside. The interior space defines a uniform, synthetic environment that knows no seasons or times of day: always the same temperature, the same Muzak, the same shadowless, fluorescent light. Time seems to have been outmoded here, just as in suburbia generally, where everything has a companionable appearance of simultaneity and newness. Even though the actual range of products—like the range of architectural options—may be relatively narrow, as compared with those the city offers, the effect is never one of scarcity. On the contrary, the reiterated sameness—of shoes and clothes and movies and food and everything else the mall contains—gives the impression of a great and inexhaustible plenty, a plenty precisely concurrent with that of suburbia.

Just as the fulfillment of suburbia need not be waited upon culturally, the objects contained in the mall are likewise approachable and undefended. Access, as a positive right, is the whole rationale for the mall, both visually and materially; it is the lesson people learned from seeing through, and abandoning, the city. That aspect of these spaces is also modeled on the suburbs from which the malls spring. Houses, like the people in them, are directly addressable: you drive your car right up to the front, ring the bell, and there the owner is, unmediated by doormen, entry ways, or waiting (for a bus, for admittance, for an introduction). The same goes for malls. They, unlike department stores, are all built to be approached easily by private car; they're located near freeways and surrounded by vast parking lots. There are plenty of signs to guide you, and entrances to let you in. The whole point, obviously, is to get consumers directly into touch with objects in whatever manner (and condition of dress and/or cultural attainment) they please. Here, the mysteries of narrative investiture have all been dissolved, so that the whole place—or as much of it as a single pair of eyes can take in at one time—offers itself simultaneously to view.

The former opacity of objects—like the mysterious power of culture and cultural institutions—is here in a state of visible disintegration. But unlike the blighted city, the mall turns transparency—for a time, at least—to democratic, utopian fulfillment. Things can be seen and touched and had just for what they are: things. There are plenty of clerks, usually, and usually they are kids, either more or less dressed up, depending on the franchises they work for, which are the same franchises you'll find in every comparable mall in every other city all across the country. Their job is to take money, not to interrogate you or your reasons for desiring one commodity as opposed to another. Whatever dreams or needs you arrive with, these will remain your own, unmolested and unadvised. No one is to feel cowed by the goods, in other words, any more than the space that contains them. Take shoes, for example. The physical overinterpretation of that category of items results, sooner or later, in the impression that everyone, *by nature*, desires new shoes, or else there wouldn't need to be so many stores selling them. And the same goes for make-up, jeans, frozen yogurt, designer cookies, fancy lingerie, and so on, and so on. Perhaps more than any other institution of "late capital," the mall stands—very precisely—for the life of objects after culture.

Despite the openness, that life is not an entirely easy one, however. On the contrary, like Gatsby's smile, the mall's transparency threatens at every moment to expose its unmysterious and undefended objects to scorn and its human occupants to a creeping disillusionment. The crisis that made the smile seem both marvelous and also threatening has itself been seen through, no less than the "culture" the smile once mocked. People grow accustomed to having paradise offered to them, on convenient installment terms; they even get bored with the idea. Thus the predicament of the shoppers in Charles Baxter's wonderful poem, "The Passionate Shopping Mall":

> . . . and there was light
> from nowhere that fell all over everything.
>
> You could tell how serious the mall was
> by the way people got lost there,
> wondering where the light had come from
> and what they had driven there to do. . . . (7)

This same sense of well-lighted disorientation overcomes the objects in Nicholson Baker's novel *The Mezzanine*, where consumer goods appear in their simple, undefended materiality. Inside the novel, no less than the mall or the suburb, time is no longer a meaningful reference. The book's "action," such as it is, involves the narrator's buying a pair of shoelaces during his lunch hour. That's all. What the book is really about is the life of objects, or more particularly the way that objects have become addressable, in themselves, within this well-lighted space where everything is so clearly seen:

> Earlier that lunch hour, I had visited a Papa Gino's, a chain I rarely ate at, to buy a half-pint of milk to go along with a cookie I had bought unexpectedly from a failing franchise. . . . I paid for the carton of milk, and then the girl (her name tag said "Donna") hesitated, sensing that some component of the transaction was missing: she said, "Do you want a straw?" I hesitated in turn—did I? My interest in straws for drinking anything besides milkshakes had fallen off some years before, probably peaking out the year that all the major straw vendors switched from paper to plastic straws, and we entered that uncomfortable era of the floating straw. (4)

What follows is a footnote of almost a thousand words in which the author describes various physical aspects of the plastic straw problem: "I stared in disbelief the first time a straw rose up from my can of soda and hung out over the table, barely arrested by burrs in the underside of the metal opening" (4), and so on. For one hundred and thirty-five pages, the novel proceeds happily in this way, engaging the reader in contemplating the familiar uncanniness of mundane objects.

The effect is very like what Fitzgerald imagines for Gatsby, following his disillusionment, though with none of the histrionic overtones: "He must have looked up at an unfamiliar sky through frightening leaves and shivered as he found what a grotesque thing a rose is and how raw the sunlight was upon the scarcely created grass" (162). The objects in Baker's mall seem likewise "scarcely created"; it is as if they are being seen here for the first time because always before something else—culture, habit, expectations of every sort—got in the way. (That this unusual book became a critical and popular success, making its way even into *Time* magazine and the listings of the Quality Paperback Book Club, attests to the recognizable familiarity of the author's uncanny contemplations.) While the novelty of these first-seen objects can be diverting, it is a novelty that—dangerously—does not sustain a lasting interest any more than Baker's ingenious fiction invites a sequel. Like Nick, who is at one moment dazzled by Gatsby's smile only to find himself in the next moment looking up, somewhat disillusioned, into the face of a "young roughneck" who only "just missed being absurd," visitors to the space of undefended objects are no less liable to having insight turn back upon them:

> Maybe it was
> the shoes. Maybe people came to see
> the clothes and the colors and felt bad
> about themselves and decided not to have
> affairs but to spend money instead. Maybe
> the mall said, "People are ugly
> fundamentally." (Baxter 7–8)

The loss of imaginative agency makes the mall disillusioning. Objects are now disabused of their cultural romance; they can be approached in unmediated form, both architecturally and also ideologically. The problem, at least potentially, is that objects thus seen through lose their transformative potential: they'll never more be able to change you into somebody else. The sympathetic light goes out of Gatsby's smile, then, and shoppers are left confronting a plenitude that speaks only of its own inert duplicity, which yields the conclusion—however consciously expressed—that "People are ugly fundamentally."

The mall's abdication of romance is just what turns social critics against it, as in the following passage from the suggestively titled, *The Malling of America*:

> The environment bathes you in sweet neutrality. . . . The sheer number of products and experiences you pay for and their apparent variety are in themselves factors that excite and focus. Once again, it's all a lot like television. TV lulls and stimulates simultaneously. The medium itself is familiar and comfortable and friendly. . . . Watching television we are everywhere and nowhere in particular, just as at the mall. Suddenly you might realize that you've been watching it all day, just floating for hours. And if you look at people watching television—especially their eyes—they look pretty much like mall shoppers: the Zombie Effect. (340)

So the mall and TV are alike culpable, with the electronic medium offering, as coverage, an informational gloss on the failure of the suburban mall to institute a genuine culture.

It is as if Gatsby's corpse had returned, now fabulously transmuted into merchandise. We—or rather critics who don't like malls and suburbs and TV—stand in Nick's place, imagining the voice of the seen-through author of our past fantasies: "Look here, old sport, you've got to get somebody for me. You've got to try hard. I can't go through this alone." Whatever the vagaries of our postmodern condition, the corpse of past representations ought not be left alone, at least critically speaking. But because of the "Zombies" we have all become, that once desirable body is not likely to be well served.

This is the point that Mumford and his followers make, and the source of their authority: they recall a past of *real* differences, when material life stood for something genuine and communicable, something other than its own transparent plenitude. And this memory allows them to see through present sham and dismiss it.

So they take up for Mr. Spinks, who is no longer here to take up for himself. In his place, there is a moussed-up kid with spiky hair. That's who you run into—out at the mall—when you go shopping for a suit in one of the boutique-style franchises that sells stylish (and expensive) men's clothes. In the display window, there are mannequins with half their heads sawed away; the simulacral posture of each is meant to show a lot of "attitude," just as you'd expect. The kid is wearing a suit himself, but the fit—like the greenish color—seems more to parody style than represent it. The cut of his pants and coat—oversized and "unconstructed"—mocks the idea that clothes are supposed to be tailored in any precisely planned way. There are television monitors throughout the store; MTV is on with the volume turned up loud enough to drown out the mall's native Muzak. The kid keeps his eyes on the screen, but he's not inattentive to his customer. He saw you when you passed through the security scanner at the door, and if you stare at him long enough, he'll come over and say, "Can I help you?" Interesting question.

Or maybe you don't go there, but to a national franchise like Saks, or a local one like Hudson's, which only survives in reduced, shopping mall versions, the once grand downtown store having ceased to exist years ago. Minus the house labels, both places stock the same brand names, more or less. But there is a notable difference in the clerks. At Hudson's, a tired looking woman in black skirt, white blouse and crepe soled shoes comes to inquire if you need help. At Saks, the dress code is rather more stringent. The clerks are all men; each is wearing a dark suit. After you walk around for a while, the one talking on the telephone finishes his conversation and idles over. He approaches with all the self-satisfied confidence of somebody whose skin is that tan at this time of year; he strokes his silk retro-look tie, reinserting its broad tip seductively into the cleft of his double-breasted jacket. He'll sell you a suit, or not. When you don't seem immediately interested, he strolls off—no hard feelings—and dials somebody else on the telephone.

Along with Mr. Spinks, the store has lost its social character. Except for credit information, there is nothing to be exchanged, nothing to be told and retold about these wares, which once became desirable—and sociable—by virtue of repeated, public narration. Whatever dialogue still occurs here is quotidian and postcultural. (Except for the woman at Hudson's, of course. She goes out of her way—mariner-like—to tell *her* tale: she's a refugee from "downtown," waiting out her pension at this forlorn spot.) The fashion choices of the clerks—like the blow-ups of magazine photographs that adorn the walls—refer to a captioning that only exists elsewhere: in *GQ, Playboy, M*, or on *MTV*. This absence of communication makes the merchandise seem at once both approachable, and also forlorn: costumes for an "obscene" play that will never be staged. As Barthes supposed, the vicarious, photogenic celebrity of the goods is parasitized—seen through—by virtue of its informational dependency, its loss of an articulate, sociable life. Pointing to the essentially conservative, or "neoconservative," nature of this exchange, Nelson Aldrich offers the following characterization in *Old Money*: "The coming of the Celebritocracy [means] . . . the role of the public has been transformed from that of a largely powerless onlooker to that of a consumer whose choices control the composition of its own 'radiant body.' This is social democracy as a form of consumer sovereignty" (47). But as Aldrich suggests, and as anyone who visits malls can confirm, suburban democracy has not rendered objects any more intelligible; it has not brought the figural "body" of culture any closer to salvation. The gains in freedom, though frequently misconstrued, have left individuals more rather than less vulnerable to manipulation.

## IV: The Life of Objects

From where I sit, in my apartment on the twenty-seventh floor, I can see a great deal of the city: the old downtown, centered around the Hudson's store; the Queen Anne mansions of Brush Farm; the Eastern Market; the "New Center," where the Fisher brothers and General Motors built their world headquarters in the 1920s; the Brewster Projects that Eleanor Roosevelt dedicated, just after the Crash, and that Diana Ross would later grow up in; and everywhere, poking through the canopy of trees, the steeples of Gothic revival churches. Except for the freeways, and the mirrored glass towers of suburbia that sit—toylike—just this side of the horizon, some fifteen miles off, the city looks pretty much as it would have fifty or sixty years ago, before anyone might have guessed what was coming. The only difference is that if I had somehow been up here then, looking out, I wouldn't have seen as much green as I do now. Great tracts of land where factories and houses and commercial buildings once stood have been retired from urban employment and bulldozed into haphazard rustication. Trees and grass grow there now, and pheasants, of course. In the fall, it's not unusual to find tumbleweeds blowing down the street in front of my building, which stands on land close to the river that European explorers first laid claim to and began fighting for three hundred years ago.

One of the largest empty spaces I look out on used to be a blue-collar Polish neighborhood where some of the workers at the old Dodge Main plant once lived. The plant, which is gone, employed 20,000 men. The city that it sustained and represented was organized by a profound faith in the production and sale of objects and the lives that those objects made possible. "Center of the most advanced industrial development on earth, Detroit is also rich in historic associations," which is how one historian began his only slightly hyperbolic account in 1951, in observance of the city's two hundred and fiftieth anniversary (Quaife ix). Nobody would say such things about Detroit nowadays for the simple reason that they are no longer true—at least not the part about "advanced industrial development." "Detroit is notorious as the American city that doesn't [work]," as *The Economist* put it recently, in a portrayal more familiar to contemporary readers:

> Flight from the city of Detroit . . . has created an eerie emptiness downtown. Within a mile of the Renaissance Centre [*sic*], Detroit's landmark skyscraper, stand hundreds of handsome red-brick houses. They are similar to the turn-of-the-century houses that fetch $400,000-plus in a gentrified downtown area of Toronto. . . . Yet the Detroit houses are worthless. They have been abandoned by their owners. Most have their windows boarded up or smashed. They have been stripped of their plumbing and other fittings. A few still house squatters: the poverty-stricken as well as drunks, whores, crack addicts and other riff-raff. The stench of urine in the hallways can be overpowering. (17)

What is perhaps most notable in such (by now) familiar representations of this place is a sense of disbelief, even horror, at the willful abandonment and destruction of so much real property. Things that are still quite valuable elsewhere—"turn-of-the-century houses that fetch $400,000-plus in a gentrified downtown area of Toronto," for instance—have here been "stripped" both culturally and actually; they are humiliated of all former significance. Undefended and "worthless," a few become the last resort of squatters, although most remain vacant wrecks. Unavoidably, there is an "eerie emptiness" about this place that once stood for all the things that industry could do and now stands for its conspicuous failure. It is as if the people who live here have forgotten what the good life means; and the ones who still remember have all left.

As to "historical associations," then, Detroit makes for pretty frightening company; it embodies an exaggerated seeing through of conventional decencies (and objects) that most people, particularly middle-class people, still cling to, nostalgically, despite the evidence of the mall. The disintegration of traditional culture that made postwar suburbia seem both possible and desirable (and subsequently produced the mall culture that sustains it) has, in the city, been carried to anarchic extremes. Here, suburban access gets turned to "obscenity"; the "passionate" ambiguity of the mall becomes unmistakably frightening in its exaggerated, urban form. This makes people want to leave, and because they leave the place seems all the more to have been seen through.

In this general state of absence, the city gets written into a kind of historical quarantine; it comes to stand only for its own, unique self-cancellation: "Dumptown Detroit," the caption added by *The Economist* editors to a photograph of African-Americans waiting in line at a food stamp center. But that doesn't mean an end to interest in this place. Far from it. Abandonment, in fact, becomes the starting point of a certain (in)human utility for the city, as I've pointed out. Detroit, in this respect, is perhaps the one incomparable city in America. Its representation in the media stands for what everyone else fears and wants to be different from: a singular, cautionary disaster from which people elsewhere imagine they still have time to retreat. But just because of that fact, this is also the most typical city of all because no other place comprehends as much as it does. All cities, to a degree, provide the millenarian inversion that Jameson talks about, the inversion that keeps alive the middle-class faith in representation, even when it has been so humiliated institutionally. But no place is better at that than Detroit.

Bad and fearful happenings are allowed to go on here—both actually and in terms of popular representations—because "Detroit" provides a scene for reporting the worst of the news and at the same time making it seem as if that news can be "dumped" or otherwise disconnected from the stories that apply to everywhere else. For example, *Time* magazine proposed the following thesis in its report of the Detroit Pistons' second consecutive National Basketball Association championship: "Perhaps because victories come so rarely, they seem to unhinge the residents of Detroit" ("Derailed by Success" 25). The report of the NBA playoffs—only eighty-nine words in length—was carried in the "American Notes" section of the magazine, with the Pistons' victory being covered in a single dependent clause. The featured sports story for the week was a page-long celebrity piece on the forty-three-year-old baseball pitcher, Nolan Ryan: "The Old-Timer for All Seasons" (68). The point was not merely to deprive this city of positive representation—news of general interest about a sports play-off, which was followed by millions of Americans—but to remind readers elsewhere that Detroit is still an incomparable dump where neither people nor property can be adequately defended:

> Each Halloween provides another excuse for Detroiters to vent high spirits, leaving extensive property damage in their wake. Last week, after the Pistons won a second straight professional-basketball championship, success once again proved more than Detroit could safely handle. In a long night of celebrations punctuated by gunfire, eight people were killed. (25)

This is not great sports reporting obviously, but it does tell the story that people want to hear—people, that is, other than the ones who still live in the city.

In this as in most other respects, however, Detroit still embodies an essential, and essentially American, kind of production: the neglectful demolition that takes place before we finally get rid of the past altogether. And that—the dumping of history—is arguably the only culture that Americans do still actively share. In particular, this is the place where Modernism finally comes to term: where the crisis of Gatsby's smile has been outlived. The smile was all about what might be, rather than what had been. And that—the being present without submitting to the narrative supervision of the past—is what makes the smile both beguiling and also vaguely sinister. So people invented a compensatory history for Gatsby; they made up stories to account for the uncanniness of his smile, or more likely to ease their own discomfort at being confronted with so much pure possibility—stories about Gatsby's having killed a man, about his being the Kaiser's cousin, about his mysterious connections. Fitzgerald understood well enough the tension that Modernism—no less than Gatsby's "greatness"—depended on: the opposing urges both to hold onto the past and to expose it as a sham. The novel's aim is cautionary in that sense; Fitzgerald is suspicious of the freedom that Gatsby invites. Here, in this city where the past has been so utterly seen through, where history—by common agreement—has collapsed back on itself like light disappearing into a cultural black hole, it's hard to take seriously any longer the crisis that Gatsby's smile once represented.

This is not to say that the city I can see from my window has been abandoned to incomprehension. Far from it. This town, like most others, has covered its historical death by translating city into city magazine. The city (as) magazine represents the triumph of suburban coverage, or more properly, it represents the triumph of suburbia as coverage: one that parasitizes the historical forms of urban culture and recuperates them as special effects. Appropriately, the city magazine scripts the intelligence of the class for whom the rituals of display are still the only available culture, but for whom the transparency of objects and institutions has become disturbingly problematical. In place of a disappeared city that no longer works, then, the city magazine comes back as pure information: instructions about eating, drinking, consuming, living a metropolitan life in general, with the categories that define this space and the discourse that informs it being once more communicable and shared. (Shared, at least in the sense that the same instructions circulate to thousands of subscriber households each month.) For that matter, the suburbanized city of the magazine has achieved the universality of the mall, of which it is the projected outcome. No city, these days, is without a magazine, and no magazine (absent its title page) is distinguishable from any other.

That is what the suburbanization of the city has meant. Historical disintegration has brought in its place a bland, textual simulacrum, which, thanks to the perfume scent strips, even smells like a mall-store on Saturday afternoon. Every city is now mapped by the same "features" and "departments" format. These, unlike the sections of a daily newspaper, can be composed days or even weeks ahead because the writing has been liberated from aleatory entanglements—local reporting, in other words. Editor's comment, letters, "Front Lines," "Media Watch," "July's Lowdown," "Discoveries," "Restaurants," "Classifieds," "Exposures" (i.e., candid party photographs): like the predictable categories of mall shops, these always already familiar "departments" anchor the city magazine and make visitor/readers feel at home, even when the city nominally represented is a foreign one.

Each magazine covers with a hipster's knowing insight the precise dissolution of differences—of race and class and culture—that once informed the city narratively and made it meaningful and unique, but that now, in abandoned form, only make it seem threatening, empty, and failed. "This century has seen a drastic expansion of mobility," as James Clifford has pointed out:

> There seem no distant places left on the planet where the presence of "modern" products, media, and power cannot be felt. . . . "Cultural" difference is no longer a stable, exotic otherness; self-other relations are matters of power and rhetoric rather than of essence. A whole structure of expectations about authenticity in culture and in art is thrown in doubt. (13–14).

The malling of difference is what the city (as) magazine is all about, as for example in the following "Front Lines" blurb (titled "Bruce in Your Face") from *Detroit Monthly*:

> [Bruce] is missing lots of teeth, his clothes are ripped and dirty, he smells like an empty house. Drivers who just miss the green light near Larned and the Chrysler Freeway may suddenly find him sprawled over their car, spraying the windshield with Windex. Depending on their outlook on urban encounters of the close kind, they either smile or grind their teeth. There are no middling emotions about The Windshield Guy. (Hopkins 14)

Here is just the sort of "riff-raff" that made Detroit seem incomprehensible to *The Economist*; Bruce even smells "like an empty house," as if to recall their worried (and all too literal minded) attempt at understanding abandonment. But despite his missing teeth and the rather bleak story he tells the writer, Bruce is served up here not as a person, but as a trope, thus illustrating Clifford's point that "self-other relations are matters of power and rhetoric rather than of essence." And insofar as the intelligence of the magazine is concerned, that is how things have to be.

Otherwise, what are we supposed to do with or about "The Windshield Guy"? Except as coverage, such "urban encounters of the close kind" remind visitors not so much of their "native intelligence," but of the homely, desperate otherness that the withdrawal of culture has exposed. For that reason, the undefended city presents the same problem as the undefended spaces of climax suburbia and its representing agent, the mall. The city (as) magazine responds, then, to the same paradoxical truth *un*covered at the mall, that access brings a loss of comprehension, and with it the threat of dispossession:

> Maybe
> the mall said, "People are ugly
> fundamentally." (Baxter 8)

In this connection, therefore, the activities of city magazines and television share a common project: a removal from the scene of potential, real "encounters" to an informational space of virtual visits. Coverage, in other words.

In most respects, and particularly with regard to the consuming of goods and services, the coverage of the magazine is concurrent with the coverage of TV and subject likewise to its insights and limitations, though the process is perhaps less sinister than Mark Miller, for example, imagines it in the following:

> Guided by its images even while he thinks that he sees through them, the TV-viewer learns only to consume. That inert, ironic watchfulness which TV reinforces in its audience is itself conducive to consumption. As we watch, struggling inwardly to avoid resembling anyone who might stand out as pre- or non- or antitelevisual, we are already trying to live up, or down, to the same standard of acceptability that TV's ads and shows define collectively. (327)

The similarity of magazine and television coverage lies in the urge —projected back from Levittown and from what we have learned in it (and beyond)—for some still viable, collective address: an unfulfillable desire to get inside TV and find company there. The isolation and disillusionment one feels in undefended visits—whether to objects or to the city that used to contain them—is covered by the hip pose of shared insight, of seeing through things. Thus the difference between a toothless beggar washing your windshield, and the sit-com-like coverage of an "encounter" with "the windshield guy." Despite the similarities, however, the visits of TV are all to a commercially generalized *elsewhere*, whereas the visits of the magazine, though no less simulacral, are to a place that people still imagine they can meaningfully call home. This makes the loss in the latter case at least *seem* more profound.

Even so, the common element remains the same: time. That is what makes the mall and the city (as) magazine distinct from the historical city that people came to understand and grow fond of by *spending time* in it. Now the flow of intelligence is reversed; absence from public space (and from its culturally narrated visits) is the basis of comprehension and security. Closing the magazine, walking out of my building and into the town, means a loss rather than a gain, precisely because of what I know, as a reader of text. Inevitably, as a pedestrian, I must give up the omniscient simultaneity of the magazine that stands in for the general, informational coverage of which it is a particular expression. The city at ground level is conspicuous for its incompleteness, its blank spaces, its danger; it invites, therefore, what de Certeau calls a "therapeutics for deteriorating social relations" (xxiv). Which is to say, the narratively decayed city gives rise to magazines that parasitize its inferior urbanity and turn it to local color. The same is true of the mall: it covers the variously thematized commercial objects contained within it just as the magazine's departments cover the city and provide it with a virtual (and distinctly unhistorical) intelligence. And just as the intelligence of the magazine is parasitic on the actual city, the implied comprehension of the mall makes each individual shop, once entered, seem less by comparison.

In Derrida's terms, the mall/magazine reader's presence in any particular space is always "traced" by the absence of all the other apparently possible choices, so that the closer one approaches the objects contained there, the less real they become:

> [Reading] cannot legitimately transgress the text toward something other than it, toward a referent (a reality that is metaphysical, historical, psychobiographical, etc.) or toward a signified outside the text whose content could take place, could have taken place outside of language. . . . What we have tried to show by following the guiding line of the "dangerous supplement," is that in what one calls the real life of these existences "of flesh and bone" . . . there have never

> been anything but supplements, substitutive significations which could only come forth in a chain of differential references, the "real" supervening, and being added only while taking on meaning from a trace and from an invocation of the supplement, etc. And thus to infinity, for we have read, *in the text*, that the absolute present, Nature, that which words like "real mother" name, have always already escaped, have never existed; that what opens meaning and language is writing as the disappearance of natural presence. (158–59)

The neologisms of Derrida's "writing" become powerful because he speaks for the paradoxical unreality that arrives after culture. Malls, like cities, expose their contents—whether objects or people—to a necessary "danger." Each provides a form of coverage the sole point of which is to tease out the supplementary unreality of its elements. That is what leads consumers to keep consuming; it leads people who already know that the city no longer exists to continue visiting and spending in it. In both cases, the "disappearance of natural presences" opens a space for the profitable—and endlessly supplementary—"writing" of commercial coverage.

But as Derrida suggests, this is a "dangerous" position. Although the supplement perpetuates desires that will never be satisfied, this endless regress—though potentially profitable—can lead to isolation and ennui, as Baxter's poem about mall culture suggests. The problem is that the reality of objects—no less than the individual who consumes or displays them—is not available locally, sociably, which makes info/serv quite different from the representational culture that preceded it. "We've lost the sense of the social life of the city as an educative process," as Richard Sennett recently pointed out; "for Americans today, the public realm is a silent realm, which is not the way it once was" (1990: 52). In place of my pedagogical visits with Mr. Spinks, for instance, one gathers information anonymously, from "obscene" surfaces: MTV, catalogs, magazines, films. It is possible to cultivate a certain look in response to this information, but recognition remains uncertain because, as Sennett suggests, "the public realm is a silent realm." You never know who is looking now, or with what level of insight and intelligence because all of us live outside the communicable, pedagogical culture of the old store. Which leads to the "voguing" that the pop star Madonna has so profitably invoked: one strikes a pose, individually, the sole point of which is to show that you are posing, to show—paraphrasing Derrida—that absent a cultural signified there have never been anything *but* poses.

This accounts for the odd way people often eye each other in public spaces, as if trying to rediscover the secret—there, in the body's surface, or in the objects and clothes that adorn it and lend it a pseudo-opacity—of some long forgotten language. The strategy, institutionally, is one calculated, as I have suggested, on the profitable exploitation of the supplement. "The signs' ultimate function," as Bogue has pointed out, following Deleuze, "is not to signify anything but to sell merchandise. Commodities, then, constitute a code whose signs exist only to sustain the code; the code regulates both commodities and consumers and thereby integrates consumption with production, completing a circuit of regimentation necessary for the maintenance of late-industrial capitalism" (131). At this precise point, then, objects and bodies converge. The internal space of each—like TV space in particular and info/serve space in general—is fully opened to commercial insight, but particularized so highly as to be both everywhere and nowhere, standing for nothing except a momentary vogue. The more you know, the more there is to worry about because there is no space now, of either bodies of objects, that is not seen into; and to remain unaware, is to be subject to errors, even danger, whether the danger is one of bad taste, bad health, bad value, or something else. Information, then, doesn't bring a release from anxiety; just the reverse: it dissolves individual agents into multiple addresses no one of which stands for finality. The aim is to maintain the object of coverage at the precise vanishing point of its own agency and to compensate disillusion with Baudrillard's "ecstasy of communication," which translates commercially into an endless supplementing of desire.

In this context, if the magazine and the mall institute a suburbanized obscenity, then information—no less than the city—has been subjected to a certain gentrification: a cultural reclamation of the too transparent state of disrepair that things have fallen into. This process goes forward textually in catalogs and magazine advertisements that make appeal to the past, which through the 1980s, has become synonymous with the discourse of high-end desire. In the past, it is possible to imagine a sociable, secure life for people and objects before either had been seen through and subjected to the access that makes life both dangerous and banal.

More brilliantly—and typically—than anyone else, perhaps, Ralph Lauren has developed this highly profitable real estate. From the beginning, his advertisements showed people in groups, but not the obscure, postmodern *situations* of Calvin Klein or Georges Marciano. With Lauren, nobody was meant to "guess" what was going on or who these people were; his layouts invite us to recognize at once the familiar tropes and players of social life. Lauren's people were obviously part of an extended and respectful family—American classics. There was the old gentleman, the young boys, the twenty-something guys, and always the wistfully beautiful young women, staring off somewhere into the middle distance, across perfect lawns, perfectly furnished bedrooms, perfectly appointed terraces toward perfectly disheveled children. The retro-fantasy was, for lack of a better word, *perfect*. And what is perhaps most important, it was shot to look like a family album, the represented record of a richly *private* life, which is why the models are recognizably the same, from one month to the next, with some of their roles lasting for years. Witold Rybczynski is undoubtedly correct in remarking of Lauren's campaigns,

> It is unlikely that anyone would ever furnish his or her home to look like the Lauren publicity brochures. But that is beside the point; advertisements often represent a not altogether real, stylized world, but one which does reflect society's view of how things *ought* to be. These themes have been chosen to evoke popular images that are informal and comfortable, reminiscent of wealth, stability, and tradition. (11)

Perhaps most important here is the notion that Lauren has captured society's notion of how *things* ought to be, which is to say, how they can be returned to a condition of sympathetic opacity. That is why his things are nearly always photographed in the company of people who obviously remember how to enjoy them. The past, as he so profitably discovered, provides a means of defending objects against the obscenity of information; this discovery has landed him not only a fortune, but also (fittingly) a historic New York mansion to call his commercial home.

An object in the imaginary past is crucially different from one at the mall—or even one in a common magazine ad—because it cannot be directly approached. The object reminds the viewer of a kind of private time that it comprehends, which is no longer generally accessible. By thus regaining control over its own interior, its memory, the object regains its capacity for secrets as well, and for conferring once more upon the owner the effect of Gatsby's smile. For example, there is the following copy from a Sharper Image advertisement for a restored Coca-Cola machine:

> 1956: Cadillacs are pink, Elvis is the rage, and every corner store and filling station dispenses America's favorite soft drink from a shiny red and white vending machine. You drop in your dime, open the door, and pull out a familiar frosty bottle. . . . **Make the memory real again.** Three-and-a-half decades later, you can still stop time with "The Pause that Refreshes." ("Own the Ultimate" 21)

The ad copy might have been written by Jay Gatsby, who has himself come in for no small amount of retro reanimation. "'You can't repeat the past,'" Nick told him: "'Can't repeat the past?' he cried incredulously, 'Why of course you can!'" (111). All you have to do is buy—in this case a Coke machine costing $7,700—to "make the memory real again."

What the gentrification of the past has meant is the introduction of a new class of objects into the informational neighborhoods of catalogs and magazines (and ultimately stores): objects that are different, and powerful, because they have moved back here from another time. The individual consumer, whose present is a contested terrain of simultaneous and contradictory addresses—spend more, save, don't eat meat, meat is real food for real people, avoid sex, be alluring, and so on—is engaged in the contemplation of a past that is apparently more coherent simply because it is too far away to be accurately remembered. But that difference is all important because it enables certain habits of recognition and credit that —because of what we now know—have become unimaginable, though perhaps no less desirable for that. Specifically, the past enables the fantasy that objects (and the people who own them) mean more than we, of course, have found out they do. "It was a game really," or so begins a retro-blurb for Gilbey's gin:

> The lighter was Sandoz, the jewelry Cartier, and a martini was the perfect accessory. . . . No disposable items here. Make-up cases, pens, watches, everything that could help describe a person were beautifully finished down to the last detail. . . . Today, personal accessories are making a comeback. Fountain pens cling to lapel pockets, timeless watches tick from wrists and elegant jewelry once again adorns necklines. ("The lighter was Sandoz" 5)

Grammar notwithstanding, the point is obvious. Gilbey's is "positioning" itself as "the Authentic Gin" by commanding a place in this self-consciously gentrified, commercial neighborhood. Conferring with the objects of retro-consuming is much like my conferences with Mr. Spinks: the captioning affords similarly private moments, the special value of which is that they take place in public; they are all pitched toward an expectable recognition. There is a great deal of difference, of course, between a department store and a magazine, between ad copy and a person, but that is not the point; it is the effect (now) that counts.

Which is to say, the real nostalgia is for representation, in itself, rather than some lost signified: the effect of Gatsby's smile, without any crisis of belief. "Every day the modern world insists that no matter how much we know, we have no control," as Leo Braudy has pointed out:

> Our common life is retold to us primarily in the form of statistics and opinion polls. Only in the past, nostalgia implies, will our knowledge mean something. Only there can we rekindle our intimate relation to time. . . . The merchandising of . . . nostalgia through objects that create a false relation to the past plays on the hope that there is somewhere a real connection, a golden bough to ease the path back to what has been lost. We can no longer believe, without irony and argument, in that American specialness that so suffused the official culture of the 1950's. But buying a knockoff of an Eames chair or tucking into a cheeseburger and large fries at the neighborhood Johnny Rocket may preserve the feeling that at least some of its trappings still have the old magic. (2.16–17)

It's not really objects, even, but the space occupied—and gentrified—by certain objects that counts. Retrospace, if properly scripted, defines a way of rethinking interiors, of restoring to consumable culture a private and potentially "magic" life. That's why the Gilbey's campaign, like Lauren's, concentrates on "accessories": relatively affordable individual purchases that entitle the owner to certain gentrifying privileges, not least of these being a right to believe again in "the old magic" that things *generally* used to confer.

The gentrification of prestige objects—most of which, interestingly, are the commercial spin-offs of high Modernism—leads to the gallery effect. For instance, these days high concept catalogs look nothing whatever like a Sears or Ward's "text." Instead, they have the appearance of a catalog that might be found in an art museum, to accompany the showing of certain "important" pieces: a *catalogue raisonné*, in that telling phrase. And in numerous instances—The Sharper Image probably being the most familiar—the success of the catalog gives rise to a commercial establishment that models in a precise way the look and feel of an art gallery. Here people and objects can once more cohabit in a space gentrified by the conspicuous presence of retro-consumables. The same relationship, essentially, is available in numerous versions: Williams Sonoma, Laura Ashley, Burberrys, Coach, Louis Vuitton. But in each instance the project remains the same, the loving enfranchisement of the past.

The gallery effect doubtless had its beginning in the "Reagan revolution," as Debora Silverman has argued. Noting the difference between a traditional leisure class, such as Veblen described, and the "corporate managers of appearance" that came to dominate the informational culture of the 1980s, she has emphasized the important role played by museums:

> Veblen's elite protected culture as a source of stability and tradition; Reagan's elite colonizes culture for consumerism. . . . The 1980s mass market moguls are cultural cannibals; they absorb the historical materials of art-museum exhibitions for the purposes of advertising, public relations, and sales campaigns. Rather than the domain in which to express the moral brake on conspicuous consumption, the museum becomes the extension of the department store and another display case for the big business of illusion making. (18)

What started out so conspicuously at the Met in New York, with such "new society" types as Ralph Lauren, Nancy Reagan, and Diana Vreeland, has trickled down just about everywhere, both socially and also textually. Gallery-look catalogs and mall shops make available, to virtually every credit-able American, a version of the entitlements of Silverman's "new aristocracy." Even here, the Detroit Institute of Arts regularly rents out space for society functions, with every member of the museum's Founders Society automatically receiving a subscription to *Detroit Monthly*, which in turn prints the current schedule of events, along with a lot of good-looking retro-ads.

Even the body—as ultimate consumable object—comes in for its share of retro entitlements, and outfitting. To a certain extent, one puts on (one's own body) the "safety" of the past, which is also its license, by adopting the look of certain pop icons, who exist now outside their particular, historical self-destruction and float free as protective, privatizing codes. Thus the popularity of such figures as Marilyn, Elvis, Bogart, James Dean, and Judy Garland, who lived (and died) before the era of personal trainers, cholesterol, AIDS, jogging, and aerobicizing. By doing Marilyn (with appropriate vintage props and accessories), or doing a greaser, you get yourself out from under the informational gaze of what you always (now) already know and into an infantilized space that is protected by its thematized naivete. But here, as with objects generally, the effect—if it is to be successful—is subject to constant renewal, a point that retro-merchandisers have clearly understood. Their upscale catalogs, then, take on the publication schedule and format of magazines because the space that each models and sells—like the space of galleries and museums—cannot be preserved and quoted; instead, it's all a matter of coverage: on/off, being in or being out.

For that reason, the coverage of the past is best experienced in private, where the atmosphere is easier to maintain and where it becomes easier, consequently, to suspend the disbelief on which desire depends. To the sequestered catalog shopper, the ability of the text to appreciate and value the past stands as a guarantee of the old virtues: quality, individual service, attention to detail. This is true even when most of the merchandise, as with The Sharper Image, does not make a specific retro-appeal. Still, the tone is established, the gentrified atmosphere assured. "This may be the handsomest Curvex of all," gushes the copy for an electrified knock-off of a 1930s watch; "order now and own the classic watch you don't have to treat like a fragile antique" (*Sharper Image* 6). That's what makes the retro-past preferable: it's a knock-off too. This is not history being offered for sale (some "fragile antique"), but the effect of history with none of the attendant bother. Thus the buyer can be assured of "authenticity" without having to sacrifice economy or technology. This scheme of synthetic assurance extends even to the first-name, personalized telephone conversations that bring the goods to the door. Objects arrive, then, as concretizations of the text, capable of extending its congenial operations into the private space of the home without the potentially disruptive interference of mall shopping.

Gentrification is not only a matter of catalogs, obviously. There are retro-coded neighborhoods in most large cities where the same effect has taken on tangible, urban form. Madison Avenue, the Near North Side of Chicago, certain parts of San Francisco and Pittsburgh, Cincinnati and Indianapolis, and countless other cities have all been made over at street level so as to provide "vintage," boutique-style spaces where a shopping experience assumes the privacy and intimate scale of a visit to someone's home, or a stroll through a catalog. In cities where actual retrieval is not feasible, there are gentrified malls, such as Somerset, which is just outside Detroit, in a place called Troy. There, one finds such stores as Rodier/Paris, Brooks Brothers, Burberrys, Williams Sonoma, Bally, and The Sharper Image. The interior design goes against all the rules of suburban mall building. This is no blimp hangar with a fountain, but a space scaled to resemble a small residential street such as used to exist here, and like ones that have been converted to commercial use in other cities. The store fronts are not typical mall entries; instead, they are made to look like the outsides of shops might have fifty or sixty years ago. There are relatively few people, and even fewer kids, because there are no movies, no arcades, no fast food joints. In terms of retro-demography, none of that stuff has happened yet, nor will it. The objects, like the generally attractive white people inside, are protected from such invasive outcomes.

So, what is there to be said for (or against) the life of objects after culture, and the body as object? And what about the antiquation of history and its replacement with a synthetic past? Is the obscene dissolving into information a good or a bad thing? And does the space of coverage portend only strategic losses, or can it be opened to tactical gains? Those are the questions that Gatsby's crisis finally comes down to.

## V: Charlie Chaplin's Roller Skates

There's a beautiful sequence in the Chaplin film *Modern Times* (1936). The little tramp—by now a fugitive—spends a night in a department store. In much the same way that the James Woods character in *Videodrome* climbs inside the representational engine of info/serv, Chaplin gets inside the store, which represents, similarly, an earlier, production-based culture. Significantly, both acts take place in the context of criminality, and both come as the result of work experience—Woods's job as a video pirate, Chaplin's as a gullible assembly-line hand. Each character is ingested by the engine of his labor—the info/serv TV set, the industrial machine—and comes out deranged. As a result, the formerly "natural" rules of society can be seen (through) in all their disciplinary arbitrariness. For Chaplin, this means playing with time and its conventionalized representation inside the department store that he is supposedly guarding. Rather than walking, respectfully and watchfully, through the carefully scripted representation of the good life, as people would do during "regular business hours," he whizzes through haphazardly on roller skates. He plays; he humiliates the store of its narrative dignity and reveals as arbitrary its embedded cultural codes. He rewrites the time-honored discipline of the store so that its formerly accusatory contents are made to behave according to his own private desires.

Chaplin's play is smart and wonderful, but it is also dated. The cultural point of attack, or defense, is no longer the same as it was fifty years ago when *Modern Times* first appeared. Specifically, there are no more department stores for the simple reason that people don't need them. As comprehensive representations of desire, such stores have given way to other agents. People's—especially middle-class people's—habits of dress, speech, and consuming are more likely to be anticipated by TV and catalogs and malls than by the classic forms of commercial staging. Production gives way to service. The narrative romance of accumulation, of having things, gives way to the romance of space—the informational management of attitude, the noncumulative articulations of *life-style.* And the crisis of Gatsby's smile is reduced to pure pastiche. We have learned a lot from Levittown, that is to say. But we have not yet mastered the question of what, if anything, this knowledge will amount to. We have learned, either more or less consciously and with either more or less contradiction, to fear and avoid the undefended space of the city, along with the objects and people abandoned in it. Moreover, we have learned to expect access and to associate it with being Americans and enjoying our "rights." At the same time, we have learned to be bored by this putative privilege.

Without trying to fix blame, or even enter into a discussion where blame makes any sense, it is possible to say that the city—in its abandoned and humiliated state—comprehends the most about the crisis that made the American century possible, and now—for great numbers of people both here and elsewhere—makes it unlivable. The problem tactically, then, is to understand that the seeing through things and the subsequent covering of what is seen through, are not ends, but openings to knowledge. Unquestionably, the great seeing through has made it possible for people to get inside things: institutions, objects, the computer, their own bodies. And once there, they make new demands based on new levels of information, some of them obviously better than others. The problem is that the further *in*side we get, the further we get away from each other.

# Violence

## Postmodernism Ground Zero, or Going to the Movies at the Grand Circus Park

*. . . it took the war to teach [me], that you were as responsible for everything you saw as you were for everything you did. The problem was that you didn't always know what you were seeing until later, maybe years later, and that a lot of it never made it in at all, it just stayed stored there in your eyes.*

—Michael Herr

### I: Capital of the Twenty-First Century

Every American city has its old, and now usually abandoned, theaters, so what makes Detroit special and therefore worth talking about? That's an easy question to answer, at least for somebody who lives here. Detroit, of course, is America's first postmodern city, and its old movie palaces model the necessary absence—as it might be called—on which postmodernism is "founded." If one is to understand postmodernism, then, it is essential to understand Detroit, and in order to do that, one must begin downtown, with the movies at the Grand Circus Park.

As per common agreement, if such a thing can meaningfully obtain in a postmodern era, postmodernism itself has to do, more than anything else, with end markers: "These last few years have been marked by an inverted millenarianism, in which premonitions of the future, catastrophic or redemptive, have been replaced by senses of the end of this or that. . . . [T]aken together, all of these perhaps constitute what is increasingly called postmodernism" (Jameson 1984: 53). That definition comes from Fredric Jameson, who has spent a good deal of his distinguished career thinking and writing about historical endings. Whether or not he has ever been to Detroit, I do not know, though the city has spent the last twenty years rewriting itself in preparation for his reading. This fact was recently noticed by *Newsweek* magazine, ever on the lookout for meaningful trends, in a story titled "Detroit's Torn Lifeline": "Every major American city has a lifeline that reflects its vitality and its vulnerability, its history and its hope for the future. . . . In the Motor City of Detroit, that lifeline is Woodward Avenue, eight lanes starting at the Detroit River and proceeding for eight unbending miles to the city limits" (59). Based upon their reading of Woodward, as representational text, the *Newsweek* writers arrive at the following conclusion: "Woodward Avenue's glory has faded, along with Detroit's auto industry; perhaps the most violent testimony to that came on Woodward when two out-of-luck auto workers drinking in the Fancy Pants saloon beat Vincent Chin to death with a baseball bat in the mistaken belief that he was Japanese" (59). Gratuity aside, Detroit has thus, by popular agreement, earned its status as the capital of "inverted millenarianism." This is the city at the end of the industrial world, narratively speaking; and violence—as the *Newsweek* article suggests—put it there and preserves its special status. And the endless repetition of violence, of the high-tech, "splatter" variety, keeps the downtown movie houses in operation.

For Detroit, the connection between violence and the civic narrative emerged as early as July 1967, when the writing on Woodward was being done by U.S. Army tanks, summoned there by the governor of Michigan to help contain the rioting that lasted for eight days and took forty-three lives. Those deaths were real and numerous enough, to be sure. (The Detroit riot was the most costly of the urban disturbances to take place that summer.) And no less real were the yearly counts of victims that made Detroit the murder capital of the country, a distinction it has retained more or less ever since: if not in fact, at least in fancy. But it is not death as such, or violence, that accounts for Detroit's postmodern status. There had been riots before, along with all the "usual" forms of urban mayhem, although not until the 1960s did the *figure* of violence overtake, and "rewrite" the city. Violent events, then, were only a means toward an end, the end being a closure for that imaginative, narrative economy by which people learned to think of the city—this kind of city—as a meaningful destination.

The modern city that Henry Ford built was founded on certain expectations—expectations that time virtually, if not actually, fulfilled. This fulfillment defined the basis, for good or ill, on which the social contract of urban modernism was concluded. Different from the stove makers, brewers, and lumber men who wrote Detroit's pre-industrial genealogy, Henry Ford democratized work on a mass scale, via his Highland Park assembly line, by reducing it to the level of duplicable idiocy. That reduction—whatever can be said for or against—is not in question here. Its results are. Narratively, Ford made the city accessible to everyone, or at least that's the way it seemed (an illusion he saw preserved, and nationalized, in his theme-park representation of America's past at Greenfield Village). In Ford's town, you could write your own ticket. For the first time, he made it appear, the common man might gain access to the good life that urban culture had for so long represented and from which he had usually been excluded. As proof, there was the fact that the great masters of industrial Detroit—Fords, Dodges, and their like—had themselves begun as humble mechanics. And now they held out —they literally represented—the promise that a life spent in work could "amount" to something. In the same way, the city in general functioned representationally; it defined a destination, where historical differences—of race, religion, language, national origin—were transformed by work into a "modern" individuality, with its common idiom of expectation and fulfillment: getting a job, buying a house, starting a family, finding a better life. At any rate, that is how things were supposed to work, and up until some point in the 1960s they actually *did* work that way for enough people to preserve the representational truth of the city.

The violence of the 1960s put an end to all that. Or, what would perhaps be more accurate to say, the violence of the 1960s demonstrated the bankruptcy of that narrative economy on which the representational value of city life was founded. When the city stopped being believable as a story—and no story was ever told in a more relentlessly single-minded way than the story of industrial Detroit—violence became the compensation: the radical, interruptive gesture whose "rhetoric" could not be refused; a desperate literalization of democracy, which (unlike the problematical good life) truly was available to everyone. Violence, then, repeated again and again, marks the end of Modernism's urban narrative, of which the present moment in Detroit's history might be looked at as a sort of epilogue. Whatever went wrong with the representational economy of American Modernism, in other words, has gone most violently wrong here.

And at no point, perhaps, does the nature of things emerge more clearly, metaphorically speaking (which becomes a more reliable medium in a postnarrative world), than at 58 Bagley Avenue, the site of the rented garage where Henry Ford built his first car. The originary garage is long gone; its likeness transposed to Greenfield Village, which is to history what the *nouveau roman* is to novel writing, except that Henry Ford's writerly text—his bunk-making of narrative—continues to be news, at least locally. In any case, the site on Bagley is presently occupied by the Michigan Theater Building, one of downtown's second-generation movie palaces built between the two world wars. But the theater itself is gone, or almost so; only the surrounding office tower remains. The vaulted auditorium has now been converted into a parking garage, so that cars sit where audiences once did, beneath the rococo ornaments that some architectural ironist has left in place. It's as if the machines, no less than their cynical inventor, saw through the bunk of representation; and now they have taken their revenge, appropriately enough, on the place where representation used to get publicly and powerfully staged: the movie theater. The transformation of that formerly significant place into violently evacuated space makes a sort of third epigraph to this essay. It is a sign in Peirce's sense: it stands for something else, the something else being the emergent *absence* of postmodernism, this absence becoming nowhere more articulate than in the movie palaces of Detroit.

## II: Crisis

As anyone knows who is up on absence, it—absence—is the fortuitous invention of commuters. What the riots did for the suburbs, the discovery of absence has done for theory and theoreticians. It has transformed crisis into valuable investment opportunities. Or to put this another way, the absence that is thrust upon the posthistorical subject is a product of intentional (though perhaps disguised) mobility: neighborhoods don't "die" until people decide to leave them, just as language only works, in a particular way, because people want it to. When things change, it is because of the choices people make. But often the choosing becomes more acceptable if its intentionality is disguised, or given some other name, so that people leave the city not because *they* want to, but to find a good school for the kids, just as the subject opts out of history not because of individual failure, but because history itself has gone wrong. This failure Jameson refers to as

> the waning of our historicity, of our lived possibility of experiencing history in some active way: it cannot therefore be said to produce this strange occultation of the present by its own formal power, but merely to demonstrate, through these inner contradictions, the enormity of a situation in which we seem increasingly incapable of fashioning representations of our own current experience. (1984: 68)

An obvious point, perhaps, but it's no wonder that history, or the city that is its product, should appear distant and strange to somebody who has chosen to live away from it, and most of whose time is spent in a place, or space so much different from this one that return becomes synonymous with disorientation.

Nor is it difficult to imagine why this type of removal has proved attractive, particularly in a city like Detroit, where the things that have gone wrong with America in general have gone so stupendously and violently and representatively wrong. But then if the accounts of the popular press are to be believed, there really is no place *like* Detroit; there is *only* Detroit, though here too the city is representative—representative of what everybody else has gotten over, or otherwise managed to avoid. "Out on the street," Michael Herr concluded, when he returned from "the war" in 1968, "I couldn't tell the Vietnam veterans from the rock and roll veterans. The Sixties had made so many casualties, its war and its music had run power off the same circuit for so long they didn't even have to fuse" (276). Detroit had its share of both in the 1960s, war and music. Whether Herr is right or not, his diagnosis developed a considerable following. Those who could afford to move away did, to get out of the city, or to escape the historical space that city life represented. Either way, the motive was pretty much the same. It became preferable to discover oneself suddenly, in a postworld, as if awakened from a troubled sleep (the literalization of which is suburbia), rather than charting the steps that led from here to there. So, it wasn't that anybody gave up; rather, it was because they'd seen through the absence of things. Absence, then, took the place of memory; it erased the lived connections that might otherwise have become responsibilities.

At this point, violence emerges as both alibi and means toward an end, which is why postwar culture overproduces, in particularly popular and vivid forms, the very thing it claims most to dread. Carefully reported incidents of actual violence, such as the Vincent Chin murder case, which the *Newsweek* editors deftly work into the headnote on their Detroit story, only serve to illustrate the reasons for getting out of town. Or there is the observance of Devil's Night, which shows just how perversely interesting a place Detroit can be. The local media are habitually pleased to report that news crews come from as far away as Japan to cover the holiday that seems to be uniquely ours. On the night before Halloween, the people of Detroit apparently turn upon their own city and try to burn it down, with the "celebration" having reached a numerical peak in 1984 when more than five hundred fires were set. I suppose it would be possible to find in Devil's Night a vengeful, correspondent literalizing of absence, by the people whom history and suburbia have left behind. Most of the fires, we are told, begin in "vacant" buildings. In any event, such destructive violence is what Detroit stands for, within the interpretant economy of postmodernism. This city has become the case of record for representing the failure of urban America.

Meanwhile, the deconstructionist project of postworld makers constitutes a sort of suburban vigilantism, launched against those who have been abandoned within the old city—or against their representational claims, at any rate, to some sort of historical authority. In a way, writers such as Jameson have done for history what the wrecking balls have done for Woodward Avenue: in the name of renewal, they have leveled the visible record of the past; they have tried to efface the trace of memory that connects an old downtown, such as ours, to the high-tech suburbs, such as lie at the other end, the desirable end, of the once meaningful narrative of Woodward.

Actually, this is going too far, in the case of both Jameson and Detroit's city planners. Each has merely executed an agenda the origins of which lie elsewhere, historically speaking. The city has apparently failed; it exists only under erasure, as one might say. But not because of any single act of bad faith, or abandonment. The city became a destination to begin with because it modeled a particular way of life that the people who arrived here wanted to believe and participate in. In the particular case of Detroit, the city mapped a life based on production, the most obvious expression of which was Henry Ford's narrative assembly line. Just like the line, the city made the individuals who served it: it organized them and got them to work; and it provided them with the necessities of life once the work was done. In this way, its chief product was a certain economy of relations: both the concrete relations on which industrial production is based; and the imaginative economy by which individuals locate themselves meaningfully in time and in a life. As a result, the city—perhaps Detroit more than any other industrial city—becomes a representational text: its form is produced by and in turn visibly articulates the way things work, as to both limits and possibilities.

In the postindustrial era of "service" or "information" this classic city no longer refers to anything real; or else the reality of things has so altered as to render the representational surface of the city a failed, aphasic relic: more an artifact than a practical text. Precisely as a text, then, the city becomes the object of reinterpretation. And in this connection, the problem of reference emerges unavoidably. "The disintegration of the sign," as Roland Barthes has said, "—which seems to be the great task of modernism—is surely present in the project of realism, but in a way that is somehow regressive, because it is carried out in the name of referential plenitude. Whereas today, on the contrary, it is a question of draining the sign and of deferring endlessly its object, to the point of radically calling into question the century-old aesthetic of 'representation'" (1978: 134). Or, to put this another way, once the plenitude of narrative production was itself rendered problematical, the modernist moment came to a close. Two recessions became Detroit's Derrida, producing the absences—the proliferating empty space—so crucial to the proleptic analysis of Fredric Jameson and *Newsweek* magazine. Now, from someplace else, postmodern "readers" feel inclined either to "defer" the reference of such signs of bad times as Detroit has become or else to deny the possibility of reference altogether.

Detroit has become (again) a city of crisis, or rather a city where the "crisis" of postmodernism—the "disintegration" of "referential plenitude"—has taken on a special, violent reality, the rhetorical point of which is an attempt to recuperate, as inverted, supervisory insight, the nostalgia for Gatsby's otherwise exhausted smile. "Woodward Avenue is Detroit," as the *Newsweek* editors were quick to conclude, and Woodward is "now a shattered memory of itself." The accompanying photographs bear this out: one from *before*, showing a bustling downtown street scene, circa 1920; the other one, an *after* image showing an old commercial building in the process of demolition. Thus the disintegration of signs that formerly constituted Detroit. In a perverse way, as these opposing images demonstrate, Detroit has fulfilled the crisis of postmodernism, turning upon itself with a fierce destructive energy that transforms the textual *place* of the city into an empty *space*, an absence, such as the gilded ruin that used to be the auditorium of the Michigan Theater, or the burnt out shells, whose emptiness the radical deconstructionists of Devil's Night have "read" and subsequently literalized.

Here the crisis of absence becomes a pervasive, lived reality: "it is a question of draining the sign and of deferring endlessly its object, to the point of radically calling into question the century-old aesthetic of 'representation" (Barthes 1978: 134). If Thomas Pynchon had been a city planner, he might have invented someplace like Detroit. "For there either was some Tristero [the underground signified] beyond the appearance of the legacy America," his character Oedipa Maas laments in *The Crying of Lot 49*, "or there was just America and if there was just America then it seemed the only way she could continue, and manage to be at all relevant to it, was as an alien, unfurrowed, assumed full circle into some paranoia" (137). That discovery comes at the end of Pynchon's novel, just as the novel itself comes at the end of a decade that has led more than one writer to seek out the creative paranoia of a "relevant," "alien" life.

Such is the nature of our present crisis, or else the nature of the postmodernist response, because in the end postmodernism is neither more nor less than what Lyotard has called it: a "condition." In that sense, even if Pynchon had been a city planner, he could never have invented Detroit because the condition of postmodernism is a matter of recognition, rather than intention; whatever has been done here was enacted on behalf of an agency, a referent, now dispersed and unrecoverable. We may check on our condition, in other words, but we are not in charge of it. Consequently, neither are we responsible for it.

This still leaves a question, however, as to who is reading, and writing, whom. "When modern critics think they are demystifying literature," Paul de Man has pointed out, "they are in fact being demystified by it; but since this necessarily occurs in the form of a crisis, they are blind to what takes place within themselves. . . . In order not to see that the failure lies in the nature of things, one chooses to locate it in the individual, 'romantic' subject, and thus retreats behind a historical scheme which, apocalyptic as it may sound, is basically reassuring and bland" (18). It becomes possible, in these terms, to read the city and criticism concurrently, intertextually, rather than allowing the one to gain authority over the other. Postmodernist discourse doesn't see through the city, then, so much as it produces a reading, a travelogue for a particular experience of urban life: the experience of a "romantic subject" as historical crisis forces upon him a failure to apprehend. This is what leads Jameson to his interest in the buildings designed by John Portman. He "reads" these structures as specially relevant renderings of "postmodern hyperspace," which consists in its effects, its having "finally succeeded in transcending the capacities of the individual human body to locate itself, to organize its immediate surroundings perceptually, and cognitively to map its position in a mappable external world" (1984: 83). This is what it means, finally, to demystify —to de-romanticize—our present, posthistorical domain.

Detroit's Renaissance Center is a Portman building: it was to recenter the comeback of the Motor City that two recessions have since effectively deconstructed. And it was to have done this in explicitly narrative terms, by teaching the affluent subjects of suburbia how to imagine their way back down town. Not to the old, failed city, though, but to the new one of glossy—if blandly reassuring—hyperspace. According to this reading, the problem is that things worked out too well. Portman recentered Detroit by revealing its total absence of center, thus the failure of the "renaissance" as both imaginative and economic venture. The structure, of course, remains, though its value is not defined in the positive terms first imagined by Henry Ford II and his fellow investors. They conceived RenCen as a place where suburban consumers would surrender to the urban romance of Gucci, Bally, and Tiffany. That never happened, and the high-end retailers have long since disappeared. In their place have come ice cream counters, sandwich shops, coffee boutiques, and other small ticket (and often short-lived) enterprises, the profitability of which is not sufficient to sustain the financial burden of the great space that they occupy. RenCen remains useful, nevertheless, although its use is now constituted in a negative way: it yields value as a written-off *absence* of profit. In a way, then, Jameson is right, though not necessarily for the right reasons.

What Jameson has failed to see, and what his deconstruction makes specifically unseeable, is that his hyperspace disorientation is itself a particular—one might even say "romantic"—kind of narrative: one that writes as universal history, or at least American history, the experience of a middle-class, suburban subject who decides one day to come back downtown, only to find that he's forgotten how to get around. Portman's buildings represent destinations, just as the classic, readerly city did, but ones (now) where the paranoia of suburbia, to use Pynchon's term, will find empirical validation: where detemporalized space is projected as general destination. The problem with this otherwise interesting enterprise is what it doesn't see: namely, all the people who never left the city; whose memories and lives are not subject to the erasure that a post-suburban architecture induces. As it turns out, these people—some of them at any rate—have discovered that the pseudo-space of the RenCen is perfectly suited to an alternate, populist discourse, which is the discourse of violence. Foot for square foot, some of the most dangerous urban space in Detroit—at least potentially—lies within the Renaissance Center, which is built on the enduringly romantic assumption that what you can't, or won't, see really does become absence.

## III: Méliès's Trick

Which returns things precisely to the movies because they have acted out, from the very beginning, the contest between seeing and believing. And likewise, from the very beginning, the movies have concerned themselves with violence, for the obvious reason that violence—even more than sex—heightens the representational crisis that makes film interesting and useful culturally. Ever since Georges Méliès discovered that he could make the streetcar in front of the Paris Opera seem to disappear and reappear merely by stopping and starting his camera, the potential of movie space has been apparent. And it is a potential related specifically to the question of seeing and believing, and the imaginative economy by which the two are negotiated. Writing of this conflict, or confrontation, Roland Barthes has maintained that

> The irreducible elements that form the residue of functional analysis have this in common: they denote what is commonly called "concrete reality" (minute gestures, transitory attitudes, insignificant objects, redundant speech). The pure and simple "representation" of "reality," the bare reporting of "what is" (or "was") appears thus as a kind of resistance to meaning. This resistance confirms the great mythic opposition between the lived (living) and the intelligible. (1978: 133)

Or to state this opposition in terms more appropriate to postmodern analysis, one might say that there exists an inevitable conflict between space and time (Jameson 1984: 64): between what the film displays, frame by frame, within the visual space; and the effect that time has in selectively transforming, or coding, the elements of that space in order to produce a "meaning." Violence, then, merely reveals a conflict always inherent in filmic representation.

For example, think of Méliès's streetcar, before confronting a more violent instance. In his brief, early film, one sees the streetcar advance, stop, and release its passengers. Because he had taken his camera to an actual and—to many in his audience—recognizable site, the "reality" of the representation, the authenticity of visual space, was assured, replete with all the aleatory "residue" necessary to guarantee its authority. But then, apparently without a break in the action, the streetcar simply disappears, as if by magic. What the spectator does not "see," of course, is the elapsed time necessary for this to take place. Méliès stopped cranking his camera, allowed the streetcar to pass, and then began cranking once more after it had moved from view. His little trick, then, reveals the collusion required between time and space if the "usual" codes of meaning are to apply. Any alteration makes a rift that cannot be accounted for except by renegotiating this coded relation. The representation of violence, by means of "special" effects, makes this point in a particularly forceful way. The screen space remains watchable only as the viewer reminds himself of the time taken out for special procedures, so that the meaning of the film is shock followed by relief (that wasn't a real head I just saw chopped off, but a simulacrum substituted for it), rather than a call to action (somebody get the police).

Both Thomas Edison and George Méliès became interested in violence early on, tinkerers that they were, so that the history of film is virtually a coincident history of special effects—special effects often undertaken on behalf of violence. Edison "executed" Mary, Queen of Scots, and Méliès sawed women in half, among other stunts. But for the time, the available technology of film making itself, together with that of the spaces in which films were exhibited, remained too crude for this aspect of the medium to be exploited fully. Also there was no particular need, historically, for either the affective ministrations of high-quality violence or the radical renegotiation of space and time that underlies the conflict of seeing and believing. That need would arrive somewhat later and with a particular relevance, demographic as well as historical, to the postmodern city of Detroit.

As Edison and Méliès discovered, the special trick of which time is capable is its ability to make blank spots in space, like the erasure of the streetcar from in front of the Paris Opéra. Time seems to be continuous, even when it is not, so that seeing puts the lie to believing, at least insofar as habit is a guide to truth. Or to put this another way, the more people have seen, the more vulnerable they become. But once the shock of having been deceived is gotten over —once Edison's viewers, for example, had assured themselves that it wasn't *really* a woman's head they saw fall into a basket, but something invisibly substituted for one—it is impossible to restore that innocence on which representation is based, or at least it takes a while to accomplish this. Violence imposes a new complexity on the *situation* of meaning, although it makes no change in the signs themselves. Because these remain the same, one thing either may or may not now stand reliably for another, and only other signs, whose reliability is itself questionable, can attest to authenticity. The situation is only rendered more problematical if the supply of signs seems to be running out, which brings up a problem special to Detroit, and to the trolley that runs in front of the apartment where I used to live.

This trolley, like Méliès's streetcar, is capable of special effects; for that matter, the trolley is itself an effect specially called into being by the things that have gone wrong with Detroit. The line is slightly more than a mile long, running from the Grand Circus Park down Washington Boulevard to Jefferson where it turns east and follows the Detroit River along to the Renaissance. The project was a local civic booster's idea for symbolizing the post-riot city's comeback. Given that context, people understandably expect the trolley to go somewhere, to reach a destination. That's the promise represented by the sign above the driver's head: spend time on this track, and you'll arrive. But in this case the promise appears to be a trick, a la Méliès. At one end of the line is the hyperconfusion of RenCen, at the other is Grand Circus Park, which is an even bigger puzzle, as far as civic representations are concerned. The Park was imagined as the center of town by Detroit's first city planners, and most main roads converge there, more or less, like the spokes of a great wheel. The Park itself remains, of course, along with the roads such as Woodward and Washington Boulevard that meet at its periphery, but other things that once made this location meaningful do not remain; and therein lies the problem, when it comes to the effects induced by a ride.

A trip from RenCen to the Park, along Washington Boulevard, serves mostly as a reminder of what's missing: Hudson's, Himelhoch's, the Statler, the Tuller, Capper and Capper, Stouffer's, Frank Brothers, the Book Cadillac Hotel, and so on. In each instance, the physical location is visible from the tracks, but what formerly occupied it is gone—not gone from the metropolitan area often (any more than the people who ride the trolley), but gone from downtown. In some cases the buildings themselves have not been abandoned, but put to other use: a women's clothing store becomes an apartment for senior citizens; a men's shop becomes a cheap coney island restaurant; people buy magazines and cigarettes where they—or someone—used to buy cashmere overcoats. In others, the spaces have just remained empty, though not unidentifiable. External walls often bear the discolored imprint of signs long since removed. Perhaps a third to a half of the storefronts on Washington Boulevard are like that. In either case, the significance of this street that the trolley runs along remains the same. Like Woodward, it used to mean something. "It was our Fifth Avenue, our Champs Elysées," or so my dentist told me, "and now just look at it."

Actually, people in Detroit spend relatively little time looking at this city, but a great deal of time remembering and writing about its past in local newspapers and magazines; this is a great place for amateur nostalgia, but not one that the majority of metropolitan residents feel good about visiting. People who have lived here for a long time are almost always glad to remember the city for me, but they're invariably dubious about my downtown address. In a telephone poll conducted by the *Detroit Free Press* for instance, 62 percent of respondents said they were afraid to go downtown. "What is there between Grand Circus Park and Fort Street," one caller was quoted as saying, in reference to the neighborhood where I lived for six years, "empty buildings?" (Soundoff 13). And that—the emptying out of this place—is precisely the problem that a trolley ride only serves to illustrate. Something like Méliès's trick seems to be going on, except in this case, it is not the streetcar that vanishes, but Detroit.

When a city is deprived of its redundancy, it stops being believable. Unless it remains capable of resisting closure, in the terms that Barthes suggests—resisting by the overproduction of its own possibility, its "concrete reality"—it will lose all credibility, just as the censored message can no longer be trusted because it has too many holes. What has happened to Detroit is that whatever used to be believable about this place—or the way that people imagined their lives here—violence has now seen through, like at the Michigan Theater, which it is now possible, literally, to see through. In a sense, then, the people who can remember the old Detroit are justified in their aversion to looking at (much less visiting) the "new" one because the more they look, the less there seems here to see, as the city comes to stand for nothing so much as its own emptiness and vulnerability.

In the postmodern confines of Detroit, memory merely isolates and victimizes, so that only people who have no memories at all—

people from outside the space or time of Detroit—will likely become interested in living here. “If there is any realism left here,” Fredric Jameson has written, “it is a ‘realism’ which is meant to derive from the shock of . . . slowly becoming aware of a new and original historical situation in which we are condemned to seek History by way of our own pop images and simulacra of that history, which itself remains forever out of reach” (1984: 71). I think Jameson is wrong about our supposedly unreachable “History,” but he is surely right about the way that Detroit has sought to reinvent itself through “pop images and simulacra.” The suburban projection of the RenCen is only one example. A more recent, and vastly more successful enterprise is that place called Trappers Alley. Again, there is the same inside/outside confusion that characterizes postmodernism, particularly as interpreted by John Portman, but with the difference that a pop version of history has now become the presiding reference of the whole project. The structure is a collage of generic markers for the past, markers that signify “pastness” while removing it from references to actual memory: exposed brickwork, old machinery, ceiling fans, fake leaded glass, and so on. In a way that the developers of RenCen only dreamed of, Trappers Alley has made “historical” Detroit both “real” and safe, so that in this simulacrum, at least, downtown has once more become a meaningful, and therefore plausible, destination.

For good or ill, the actual city is not subject to such reinvention; it remains concrete, distinct, particular, even in its failure. There—outside the developer’s hyperdome—the former collusion of space and time is repeatedly, and characteristically, interrupted by violence: the violence of the city’s own self-demolition and the individual violence, or the expectation of such violence, that now defines the emptiness that is left. Just as it is unsafe to be in a special effects movie, it is unsafe to be in Detroit, because the more you feel at home, the more likely you are to become a victim. But there’s one obvious and crucial difference. Viewers can take themselves out of the film, which is always after all *only* a film, but it is not so easy to get out of Detroit.

On a spring day, several years ago, I walked out the door of my building on Washington Boulevard. The trolley had just stopped in front, as it always does, before making the return trip to RenCen, which takes place every fifteen or twenty minutes. Two elderly women, nicely dressed, with hair the color now usually referred to as "blue," had just gotten off. Both looked frightened. It was just after lunch; the sun was shining; a few office workers were out taking the air before returning to their desks. The two women approached me. "What are we to do now?" one of them asked. I wasn't sure what she meant. "I beg your pardon?" "The conductor told us that we must wait fifteen minutes before we may return to the Renaissance, and we don't know where to go." I suggested they might walk around or else sit on one of the park benches and just wait. "But won't we be killed?" Statistically, the chances of that are about the same in my part of town as they are in Ft. Lauderdale or Honolulu; and when you take into account a few additional factors, such as time of day, and the two "subjects" being white women (as opposed to African-American teenagers, say) fearful of attack by an unknown assailant (as opposed to a friend or family member), their chances of survival increase exponentially.

I don't recall what I said to the women at that point; I think I may have offered myself as evidence that life downtown is possible and even generally safe. I know I didn't try to impress them with statistics, which I doubt would have meant much anyhow. In either case, the question they were led to by their trolley ride was not one that I was going to be able to answer because it is not so much a question as a statement of identity—an identity based on the postmodern, and posturban, individual. And for such individuals, the place of History has been turned forever into a space of confusion, paranoia, vacancy, and loneliness. "Wrong end of the line, the Renaissance is back at the River," I might have said; or "Forget what you remember, and then maybe you'll be able to see where you are," which sounds more eloquent. But they were already frightened enough. Or better still, I might have suggested that we go to the movies: not in the micro theaters of RenCen, but in one of the faded palaces on the Park. That's the real jumping off place for postmodern tourists, the kind of place where you'll only run into natives: where "History" gets staged and restaged, in the usually violent terms required to displace that classic—one might call it a "readerly"—economy of time/space relations on which the traditional, centered city depended. You don't have to wonder what has happened to Detroit, in other words, because it is still going on, for all to see, there in the dark. But both women were "from Detroit," as they put it, which is what people here often say when they mean that they moved to the suburbs in the 1960s or 1970s like "everybody" else. Because they were "from" here, they knew (because they remembered) what this place had been, so that after the disappearing act of their trolley ride, neither of them realized there was still anywhere left to go. And in some ways, that's just as well because I'm sure they wouldn't have liked the show.

## IV: Movie Palaces

All cities have movies, of course, and movies about violence, just as most big cities also have old theaters. The thing that is special about Detroit's old movies—just as with the city itself—is their postmodern situation. Things have not always been special here, however. Initially, the story of film in Detroit was altogether typical, though no less violent for that. The first film was shown in 1896, at the old Opera House on the Campus Martius: a multireel depiction of a Mexican bullfight. According to contemporary accounts, the exhibition was not particularly successful. A more favorably received screening followed when *The Great Train Robbery* was shown around the corner at a place called Wonderland, which also booked such attractions as Tom Thumb and Jumbo the Elephant. Other exhibitions followed, apparently; the first theater devoted specifically to movies opened in 1905, in a converted variety house (Woodford 226, 238). That was the Casino, on Monroe Street, not far from the Opera House (Ferry, 323). Such conversions, along with proliferating "nickelodeons," had established a theater district, of sorts, within the next few years. The majority of these establishments were located in the same neighborhood around the Campus Martius. This era in the development of local cinema was both haphazard and again typical of a general uncertainty as to the status of movies and consequently the proper means of their exhibition, so for the time they were consigned to the ambiguous domain of burlesque halls and chop suey houses.

Not until Detroit began transforming itself into the Motor City did it get serious about the movies, nor did it need to. In his novel about the history of this period, E. L. Doctorow makes a crucial connection between industrial production and the production of images. "The value of the duplicable event was everywhere perceived," he says, paying special attention to the use made of this fact by Henry Ford (1975: 111):

> Henry Ford had once been an ordinary automobile manufacturer. Now [at the invention of the assembly line] he experienced an ecstasy greater and more intense than that vouchsafed to any American before him, not excepting Thomas Jefferson. He had caused a machine to replicate itself endlessly. . . . Ford established the final proposition of the theory of industrial manufacture—not only that the parts of the finished product be interchangeable, but that the men who build the products be themselves interchangeable parts. (1975: 112–13)

This duplicability of humans, events, and motor cars leads necessarily to Ford's much-quoted view of history: that it is "bunk." The ideal worker, just as any other interchangeable part, was one that standardization had effectively dehistoricized, one not bound to any specific time or place, who could move around freely, wherever needed.

The social and economic mobility that resulted from this mode of production is what makes possible, and at the same time necessary, the next generation of movie theaters, the first of the great "palaces." Concurrent with Ford's assembly line, the point here was "screening out the past," to quote the title of Larry May's study of the early movies. Viewers—particularly such new arrivals as had been attracted by the promise of Ford's $5.00-day, which came in

1914—could trade in past differences of class, nationality, language, memory for the duplicable community of film images. In the theater, and especially in the centered theaters that grew up in the 1920s, the promise of prosperity became a lived, however momentary, reality. For a price of around fifteen cents, which practically all working people could afford, the "palace" became freely accessible; in fact, it invited entry in a way that no other social institution could, or would. There, even the humblest worker could command the markers of wealth and status. And situated with reference to such markers, the "photoplay" itself defined a "culture" that was the property of no single class or group, a culture with no past, which belonged equally to anybody with the price of a ticket: the virtual representation of America's democratic ideal that you could have whatever you were prepared to work for.

Henry Ford's first assembly line opened in 1911, in Highland Park, and by 1917, the success of that operation could be measured —and managed, at least in part—by the nine regular film theaters then advertising features. By this time Detroit was in the process of getting its first real theater district. The scattered nickelodeons and converted variety houses of earlier days were being superseded by large, up-scale buildings intended specifically for the exhibition of films, and these new establishments were no longer consigned to the company of cut-rate clothing stores and variety emporiums. Instead, they were consolidated in a more exclusive and solidly middle-class area around the Grand Circus Park, where the theater district developed and remained, appropriately, until the 1960s migration away from the city outmoded and finally killed it. The Park offered a natural environment for the large movie houses because it lay at the center of Detroit's street railway system, which was itself connected to an extensive regional network. Unlike the anachronistic trolley in front of my building, the railcars (and then later the busses and automobiles) really used to take you somewhere. Contemporary maps of the various lines make the city look like an enormous English dartboard, with the area around the Park as the bull's-eye (Schramm I: 112–13). And for fifty years, at the center of the park, what centered the city was the movies: a metropolitan "circus" providing at once both entertainment and a destination for the people who came here to see what this ultimately "duplicable" city was about. The first generation of theaters included the Madison (1916) and the Adams (1917). Next came a grander and much larger group of houses: the Capitol (1922), State (1925), Michigan (1925), United Artists (1928), and Fox (1928). All these, except the Adams and the Michigan, were the work of C. Howard Crane, who built his national career as a theater architect by building the theater district of Detroit.

As the maps suggest, there is perhaps nowhere else so relentlessly centered a city: centered economically, geographically, and centered popularly around the movies. Nor is there a city more central to what people now imagine to have gone wrong with urban, industrial America, which is what lends Detroit its special relevance. Consequently, this place, or this kind of place, becomes the object, more than any other, of postmodernism's erasure. If people are ever to get over the past and on with, or into, the future, Detroit has got to go. And that's what the two frightened women in front of my apartment building were trying to do, in a way. They were trying to take back Méliès's trick, or else reverse it: by returning the city to empty space, they were trying to dissolve the bad time it represents. If there is nothing here, after all, then there's nothing to be afraid of, or subject to.

In their anxiety, they were certainly not alone; on the contrary, they find themselves in excellent, and increasingly numerous, company. Whether it is frightened tourists, or such futurologists as John Naisbitt, the judgment remains the same: a judgment *for* the future and *against* Detroit, or the kind of centered history that Detroit represents. "We are living in the *time of the parenthesis*," as Naisbitt has said, "the time between eras. It is as though we have bracketed off the present from both the past and the future, for we are neither here nor there. We have not quite left behind the either/or America of the past—centralized, industrialized, and economically self-contained. . . . We are clinging to the known past in fear of the unknown future" (1984: 279). By instituting an economy of space, or "hyperspace"—the parenthetical betweentimes of Naisbitt's best-selling *Megatrends*—analysts expose as valueless the failed, narrative currency of a city like Detroit. And while it may be only "human" to cling to our bankrupt past, such nostalgia becomes progressively self-destructive, which is their point in writing, and the source of their rhetorical conscience: "To reach our full potential as individuals, as companies, as a country, though, we need a vision. People want to make a commitment to a purpose, a goal, a vision that is bigger than themselves—big enough to make them stretch and grow until they assume personal responsibility for achieving it" (Naisbitt and Aburdene 1985: 255). In this context, it is altogether in the interest of progress that the past be rendered frightening and chaotic because otherwise people might continue clinging sentimentally to it, thereby delaying their removal to the future.

There is a paradigm locally for this attitude: the city justifies the tearing down of abandoned, though still habitable structures (rather than giving them up to homeless "squatters") because such buildings are said to offer potential hideouts for dangerous criminals. Never mind the fact that the buildings would no longer be abandoned (and potentially dangerous) if homeless people were allowed to live in and improve them. If we're to have a new Detroit, first we'll have to get rid of the old one, and those with their sights fixed forever backward will never have a "vision" of what could or should be. In the name of the common good, then, civic, corporate, and critical entrepreneurs all urge the same thing: the dangerous antiquation of history and all those places associated with it. Instead, they argue for a present based on the alternate agenda of renewable space. It is a mistake, however, and a dangerous one, to assume that *space* either offers a real solution to historical problems or provides a source of useful intelligence. As the example of the RenCen shows, the imposition of synthetic space on the old, centered map of history doesn't solve anything; it merely submits residents to unexpected and apparently unintelligible danger. And in any case, this idea of space is nothing new. The city, like the movies at its center, has always been based on the collusion of space and time, or more accurately on Méliès's trick, which is the ability of space to render time selectively "invisible." Inventing a new space to supplant an older, failed one may be appealing and even profitable, as Trappers Alley has shown, but it does nothing to render intelligible, much less to resolve, the presiding conflict that expresses itself as violence.

Contrary to postmodernism's guiding assumption as to the recent primacy of space (Jameson 1984: 64), the quality theaters that grew up around Grand Circus Park always existed primarily as spaces: spaces for containing and administering the duplicable events of film imagery. This is what made them different from such haphazard establishments as Wonderland. The production of theater space had now become a matter of intention and design—a duplicable necessity, as the success of C. Howard Crane's architectural firm demonstrates. As such, these theaters were materially overinterpreted in the precise, textual sense referred to by Barthes in his discussion of classic realism: "the loss of the signified solely for the advantage of the referent becomes the very signifier of realism" (1978: 134). Thus the essential character of architectural referents, which are meant to refer to nothing: nothing, that is, except for the reality of reference-making in general. For example, the theaters were decorated with a profusion of objects, coded by the popular discourse of publicity, as markers of class distinction: paintings, oriental rugs, urns, vases, fresh flowers, elaborate metal work, plush, gilt, and so forth; all the superfluous acquirements of "success."

But in no case did these objects refer to anything aside from their own plenitude and presence. There is, for example, the following contemporary account of Crane's most opulent creation, the Fox Theater, which was completed in 1928:

> Few specimens of architectural splendor, either ancient or modern, surpass the new Fox Theater. Temples to gods and palaces for kings, through long years were the only outlets for architectural dreamings —until the significance of art in daily life became manifest and pervaded the buildings of intimate use. This tendency, entering the field of motion picture exhibition, has resulted in the creation of palatial buildings, an outstanding example of which is the Fox. . . . The theater itself is a wonderland of continental treasure, embracing, as it does, the salient features of Burmese, Hindu, Persian, Indian, and Chinese architecture all deftly blended into an ultra-

> modern American adaptation of the Hindu temples of old. (Ferry 325 n.12)

Here the significance of art is brought home to "daily life," and what art turns out to signify has very little to do with art and a great deal to do with the situation of those who are able to command it: whether actively, in terms of the architectural agency responsible for the theater, or vicariously, by virtue of becoming a "patron."

In either case, the "continental treasure," like the space that contains it, is not meant to be read in relation to time; the aim is not the representation of some coherent, historical signified, as the polyglot nature of the design makes clear, combining as it does "the salient features of Burmese, Hindu, Persian, Indian, and Chinese architecture." On the contrary, the function of such ultra-modern adaptations was to thematize the art of consuming itself, and to demonstrate the imperial competence of acquisition in its triumph over substantive difference, whether social, cultural, or historical. Theater space, then, does not refer; instead, it contains. Inside it, a person might economize imaginatively the seriousness of duplication and possession, as such. Significantly, the Fox did not contain "original" pieces; all its art was imitation, but imitation produced at great expense, by an army of hired artisans, whose activities reproduce the activity of film image-making itself. The making of the theater, like the making of the images inside it, represents the application of the latest, "modern" technology to the task of reproduction. In both cases, the "culture" that institutes such achievements is centered on what Doctorow calls the "value of the duplicable event." Frame to frame, feature to feature, week to week, that's why the audience came: to renew the imaginative contract of consuming on which the space was founded.

As industrial Detroit prospered, it came to need such spaces. Concurrent with the construction of the second-generation movie palaces was the building of Detroit's Institute of Art, which took place in the late 1920s. The city's collection had outgrown an older museum located on Jefferson, near the commercial part of town. Just as the theaters moved, so did the museum, which relocated in a newly conceived "cultural center," that was linked to the Park by Woodward Avenue, and by a more or less continuous string of lesser theaters and nickelodeons that culminates in the achievement of the Grand Circus.

The brick of the original museum was replaced with a "continental" design much like that of the downtown movie palaces and similar (at least on the inside) to the simultaneous architectural consolidation of the various structures that comprise the J. L. Hudson Company, Detroit's quality department store. In each instance the building, like the movie palaces, does not signify outside itself, as a romanesque or gothic design might do; its purpose is to be discovered internally. There, the "salient features" of history emerge as a code capable of consolidating and valuing a patently disparate assembly of objects and images. Space becomes a stand-in for the now abandoned "bunk" of historical reference; it accounts for the objects moved into and out of it in a way that neither memory nor mere representation could ever do, so that the desire for objects is transformed from a mere acquisitive urge to a necessary, and necessarily centered, part of culture. And this culture is itself justified by virtue of its power over the valuable objects that it is able to call to its service: the greater the range of differences contained, the greater the power of the culture that contains them. That capacity constitutes the simultaneous modernity of museum, department store, and theater. Likewise, the same cultural imperative gives Henry Ford the right to uproot such sited structures as the Wright Brothers' bicycle shop, Edison's laboratory, and Daniel Webster's house so that they might be moved to Greenfield Village (opened in 1929) where their contemporary meaning can be understood.

In each instance, the practice of such classic space comes very close to Jameson's notion of pastiche, which turns out not to be distinctively postmodern at all. At this point, then, the limitation of postmodernist thinking becomes clear, along with its self-preserving ends. Like John Naisbitt, who capitalizes the same temporal breakdown, critics such as Jameson offer the solution, or salvation, of criticism as such. In his study *The Post-Modern Aura*, Charles Newman has made the following apt comment on what might be called the multinational "moment" of literary theory:

> The attempt to assert literary criticism as *the* presiding and autonomous discipline, to usurp the prerogatives of both art and philosophy, only accentuates the fact that the culture now operates well beyond any literary frame of reference. . . . Far from providing an equilibrium of objective relations, the contemporary critical impulse pushes one beyond a consideration of transmitting culture, to breaking it up and making it over in one's own image—hence the semi-hysterical attempts to erase whatever distinctions remain between criticism and literature. (121–22)

Hence, as well, the suburban strategy, as I have called it, that characterizes so much contemporary writing and thinking about the city and the historical experience represented by such old, centered cities as Detroit.

Although this response is understandable, and like the suburbs even congenial in many ways, it is not necessarily laudable. Moral arguments aside, however, perhaps the central problem with such postmodernist thinking, as Newman suggests, is its intellectual failure. The city "knows" more—and specifically more about absence, and the violence that follows upon a confrontation with absence—than the critics who claim to have discovered, from outside, the vacancy and danger of urban experience. But the "semi-hysterical" discourse of suburbia is not really intended as an analytical instrument, regardless of its claims to civic awareness. By means of a permanent, figural crisis, those who have moved away seek to justify their abandonment of the past and to institute the kind of zoning that will preserve the value of present investments, in this instance the privilege of literary forms of analysis. In the name of intelligence, then, postmodernism abandons whatever it is not predisposed to accept or else writes it into inarticulacy. Interestingly, however, those left behind, the ostensible subjects of postmodern "schizophrenia," turn out to be neither mad nor subject to the custodial discourse that would administer their fortuitous condition. This fact emerges perhaps nowhere more clearly than in the old downtown theaters, now left to the people whom post-history has abandoned in them.

## V: Going to the Movies

Here the "bunk" of theater space demonstrates eloquently, and popularly, the "absence" that once centered the city and that now drives it toward violence. This final destination did not become clear, however, until history had run out—history of the sort that Henry Ford rolled off his assembly line, along with the Model T's. In this context, the duplicable plenitude of the department store and the movie theater both modeled—and centered—the same experience of urban life. The panoptic accessibility of these spaces was essential: everyone could see all that the space afforded, along with the differences that separated one class of objects, or spectators, from another; and they could also "see" the fact that they were there, along with everybody else. The Fox Theater, for instance, could accommodate 5,000 people in an auditorium with a view unobstructed by columns. In such a theater, there were different prices of admission, depending on where a person sat, just as a department store contained different grades of merchandise, from the finest to "bargain basement" items. (The "basement" at Hudson's dates from the late 1920s, just like the theater district.) As the city developed, with downtown reaching its economic peak in the 1950s, these internal differences gave rise to different classes of stores and theaters, each associated in turn with a particular class of objects and consumers. The first movie palaces gave way to the newer and gaudier ones, and like Hudson's basement store, the older houses began advertising themselves as "bargain" venues, with quick access to main transportation routes. In each case, however, the stores and theaters were still located within the same downtown, where they remained mutually accessible and in visible proximity to each other.

Such free access to difference would doubtless have proved problematical were it not for the second feature of urban production—mobility. The work that brought people to the city also afforded them the economic means that could translate difference into success, labor into the objects of desire. Difference remained central to the city, then, because without it the discipline of narrative production would have remained impossible and its subjects inarticulate as to the representational meaning of work and the progressive narrative of successful accumulation. In this connection, the space of theater, museum, and department store became believable because these spaces took seriously the same objects, the same way of situating oneself in relation to objects, that defined the culture of production generally. It would be a mistake, however, to approach the reality of modernist production nostalgically, in terms of a narrative history that has now, sadly, been lost. The dissolution of time and the overvaluing of space was at the center of this life from the very outset. Space, or the sharing of space, could make time disappear, so that the worker didn't think of his visit to the theater, for example, as representing so many hours of labor, but as a cultural experience that redeemed the work and made it worthwhile.

Not until the post-Vietnam failure of American production did the common space of the culture become historicized and at the same time violent. Once the dream of plenitude ended, the markers of difference became just that: indicators of a separate and permanently unequal status that no promise of mobility would one day redeem. At that moment, when mobility failed, the free accessibility of urban space made it suddenly dangerous because there the differences that defined cultural privilege were immediately available and therefore offered clear objects of attack. This situation contrasts markedly with the 1930s, when economic failure did not produce the violence and urban flight characteristic of the 1960s and 1970s. Then, hardship seemed pervasive, rather than selective: stockbrokers were (at least representatively) no less subject to ruin than common working men. As a result, the markers of success retained their talisman-like power over people's imaginations, so that *Gold Diggers* movies, for instance, were fantasies about hope, rather than invitations to class hatred.

The economic downturns of recent times have not been like that, however, with such popular designations as "rustbelt" and "sunbelt" being characteristic of the selective and exclusionary discourse of postindustrial America. We're no longer in this together, whether togetherness is defined economically, socially, or geographically. As

John Naisbitt says at the conclusion of *Megatrends*, "The North-South shift is irreversible in our lifetime. What is unclear is how the country will adjust to the changes. . . . The burden falls most heavily on the cities where change is greatest, such as Detroit and Houston" (1984: 282). Given this "popular" agenda, differences easily become exclusionary boundaries; the markers of success no longer represent a common fantasy, but a flaunting of the sunny, good life before the rusty faces of those whose lives have turned permanently bad. Thus the ambiguity of contemporary desire multiplies, becoming easily entangled with hatred and violence.

Just as theater space had modeled urban space during the era of migration and industrial progress, it similarly modeled the experience of postindustrial violence, and the concomitant transition to a "service" or "information" culture. The duplicable events of film imagery offered no greater security than historical ones since technology was now in a position to capitalize film's potential for violence in ways that Edison and Méliès could only dream of. Movies such as *Bonnie and Clyde* (1967) and *The Wild Bunch* (1969) did for the screen what the urban riots did for the streets: they ended forever the popular illusion of safety.

The change began in Detroit's theaters in the 1960s, but it was assured in the mid-1970s by a locally decisive legal case that challenged the exclusive right of the old downtown houses to first-run films. Thereafter, such films could open in the suburbs, where they were both more convenient to a specialized clientele and beyond the reach of threatened urban violence. At this point, violence enters the theaters just as it enters the culture. In a sense, it *becomes* the common culture of America, if we could be said any longer to have one. Violence also became the salvation of Detroit's old downtown movies—those that remained in business, at any rate. Without *Halloween* and *Friday the 13th*, and a host of similar though lesser known films, downtown would long since have ceased to have any theaters at all. But because downtown remains—no less a reality than the suburbs—the theaters remain, and inscribed within them is the history that both postmodernism and *Monthly Detroit* have preferred to write as absence.

In an article on the city's theaters, *Monthly Detroit* failed to mention that any exist within the city limits, on the assumption that people who know what's what know enough not to go downtown for a film. To a certain extent, the magazine is justified in this exclusion. There is no longer a market for the old, centered movie palaces like the Fox, which as everyone here knows, has gone out of business anyhow, except as an occasional venue for rock concerts. Such performances, along with high school graduations, are the only business that goes on now in the second-generation palaces at the Park. A real estate developer has bought the Fox and its neighbor the State; he hopes to make them the center of a revived theater district. A couple of years ago he tried to get the revival under way with a classic film series, but the series failed to attract an audience. The problem, I suspect, is that the State, where the series was held, still looks more or less as it always has. But because there are no longer any subjects capable of needing the centered experience represented by such a large theater, the effect must have been more puzzling than entertaining, so that the project collapsed under the deadweight of its own anachronism.

That has not been the case with all the downtown theaters, however. Of these, two are still doing business, the Adams (1917), which is among the first theaters built on the Park, and the Plaza, which is a comparatively late arrival, dating from World War II, when it opened to show movie newsreels. Until recently, the Madison (1916) was also open; it has since fallen victim to a failed heating system and real estate speculation. Unlike the larger, later palaces, these theaters changed with the times. Gilt moldings and art nouveau fittings continue in evidence, but they are covered over and partially obscured by several layers of subsequent reinterpretation, the most recent looking as if it dates from the late 1950s or early 1960s, except for the installation of video games, which brings everything pretty much up to the present. Like the theater spaces in general, the screens have also been written on visibly by history, so that during any film there are always two simultaneous texts under production: the one being projected onto the screen, and a second one being projected by it. If one were on the lookout for metaphors, deconstruction might here be seen to take on a weird spectral reality, thanks to certain stains, rips, and backstage lights that are always already playing havoc with the onscreen presences. But metacriticism or no, there's still movie business to be done at the Park; often there are long lines of people waiting to get in, particularly for afternoon shows. And these shows are almost always the same kind, with the current offerings being typical. Today, at the Adams you could see *Nightmare on Elm Street 2* and *Krush Groove*; at the Plaza you could see *Commando* and *Death Wish 2.* Fixed permanently on the marquee of the defunct Madison are *Dead Zone* and *The Keep,* which together might constitute a second meta-comment on the post-history of film at the Park.

Tom Wolfe coined the term "porno-violence" in the late 1960s to describe the sort of postmodern splatter movie that makes a lot of money downtown (1967: 59). And in other places too, although few cities have been prepared geographically to situate violence at their historical center in the way Detroit has, and few perhaps have needed to, which is what it means to be America's first postmodern city—a distinction that can only be discovered, after the fact, rather than achieved intentionally. Wolfe dated the advent of porno-violence with John Kennedy's assassination—or rather with the endless televised and printed reproductions of Abraham Zapruder's film showing the president's head exploding. That's when we lost control, according to Wolfe, of a coherent point of view: no more good guys or bad guys; only the question of who gets to be on the sending end of whatever violence is being produced by the media and by the imitative agents of popular film. Technology itself becomes the main character, the point of identification, which is only fitting in an information society; technology situates the subject reportorially, in a position of power and control. The more graphic the exploitation of objects (objects such as the now literally fragmented characters of the splatter plot), the greater the sense of mastery that accrues to the spectator.

What Wolfe discovers, then, is a radical decentering that makes the pre-1960s *then* different from the post-1960s *now.* And of course there is a difference: one has only to go downtown, to walk along the failed lifeline of Woodward Avenue, or to stop in for a movie at the Park, for that to become clear. The center obviously did not hold. But the letting-go does not originate with Kennedy, or Vietnam, or with the first postwar recession. The cultural misrecognition of the individual and individual positions has been going on for quite a while, at least as far back as the building of the first theaters at the Grand Circus Park. But until recently, the technology of misrecognition (utopian or otherwise) had not become so fixed and exclusionary with respect to differences of class and race. Such fixing, or the knowledge that it has taken place, inspires violent responses surely. But it can also become the basis of a critical intelligence: a native postmodern consciousness such as emerges in the old movies at the Park, rather than the one that gets projected onto downtown from the vantage of suburbia.

There, in the movies, Méliès's trick has finally and permanently been seen through, just as it's possible to see through the film image itself, right to the stains and rips in the screen and the bricks of the backstage wall. In the old days, theater space worked, as imaginary center, because it could make time seem to disappear, just as Méliès did when he stopped cranking the camera until the streetcar had passed. Within the democratic fantasy of theater space, everybody was an equal with an equal claim to the images of culture, even though some people had to invest a great deal of time to pay for their trip, while others had to invest comparatively little. But that, like the lost moments of Méliès's little film, ceased to matter. It is the *virtue* of theater representations, just as it is the virtue of our representational democracy, that belief is not contingent upon actual possession; rather, such representations stand for what might (and in representative cases does) become possible sooner or later: the poor man becomes president, the manicure girl becomes a movie star, and both realize the virtual promise of theater space. And the visually realized anticipation of such achievements could be hired for an hour or two at the Madison, or the State, or the Fox. Problems arose, however, when *sooner* turned out to be a much longer wait than some had expected, and *later* turned into *never* for large numbers of people who came to cities like Detroit in the years following the great democratic victory of World War II. By the present, postmodern moment, then, history seems to have written the lie of Méliès's trick all over the disintegrating theater screens downtown, just as it has written and fixed the lives of the people who sit there, in the dark.

By this, however, I don't mean to imply that theaters like the Adams have ceased to function. On the contrary, the theaters on the Park work pretty much as they always have, except that history has radically altered and evacuated the city they continue (now as postmodern anachronisms) to center. In the temporally deconstructed spaces at the Park, the people who live here gather still, in order to find out and participate in what is happening to them and their lives. The audience is genuinely representative, in a way that few other theater audiences are: there are old people using canes and walkers, children, teenagers, whole families, kids out on dates, young mothers with small children, women in twos and threes. Watching a film here is an unusual experience. The auditorium never gets really dark, and there's a good deal of movement and talk, although the effect is not particularly disruptive. It's like watching TV in a group of people, with the nominal entertainment demanding neither more nor less attention, apparently, than the average sitcom or cop show. For the most part, the people here are intent on having a good time together; the film merely introduces an occasional source of diversion and comment. But the film is still central to what is going on; after all, the audience keeps coming back and paying admission week after week. Not just any kind of films succeed, though. For the purposes of centering postmodern Detroit high-tech violence works like nothing else, and for good reason.

In narrative terms, the most obvious thing about the produced and now abandoned downtown of an old city such as Detroit is the mimetic literalizing that has been undertaken, by both residents and those who left. There is an apparent wish, which often becomes violence, to make the city appear as it actually is: to expose, in other words, the lie of mobility, which was always, finally, a lie for the majority. So, it is no wonder that public transportation doesn't work and that nobody expects it to; or that Detroit has a de facto segregated bus system: one for the residents, and one (of a different color, literally) for the suburban commuters; or that the former lifeline of Woodward Avenue got rolled up behind the post-riot migrants, now sequestered at its other end. Nor, perhaps, is it any wonder that violence of a sort that René Girard might find "ritual" should take place in the faded theaters at the city's center.

I'm reminded here of an odd postcard that I once received as a gift. It reproduces a photograph taken at the Grand Circus Park just about the time the Madison and the Adams theaters were being built. The photographer stood out in the middle of Woodward across from the David Whitney Building; he pointed his camera south, toward the river, and snapped the shutter. There's a good deal of traffic in the picture: streetcars, automobiles, and quite a few pedestrians. It's the pedestrians who make the card interesting; the face of each one has been whited out so that nobody has any recognizable features. The point, I suppose, was to erase the identity of anyone who might have objected to appearing, unawares, on a common postcard. Decorum forced the photographer to produce these oddly defaced images. In another way, though, the picture is an accurate representation because only by virtue of absence did the city become a meaningful destination. The postcard shows nobody's face, but it also therefore provides the blank surface onto which *virtually* anybody's face might be projected.

But this was a fantasy based on choice. If postmodernism has any meaning historically, then the removal of choice is surely it. That is what the radical fragmentation of the modernist subject amounts to: the loss of the self that used to be the source of intelligence and volition, a loss memorialized in the splatter film. And the lack of choice is precisely what constitutes the audience at the Adams and makes them the most postmodern subjects of all. Just as events have imposed themselves on the city, the theater imposes itself on the people inside, allowing them no choice but to see through the representations that bring them together, clear through to the rips and stains on the screen, and the blank wall behind. And that's where the story might end if it weren't for one final development that occurs in such unrestored places.

There the predicament of postmodernism gets turned into a communal gag, because what the people seem to have found when they have finished seeing through everything else (as they are compelled to do) is not the atomized world of middle-class theory, but each other. Contrary to expectation, it's precisely the seeing through that defines this audience and brings them together, which is why people keep coming here week after week. Far from making their exposure and the consequent prospect of violence seem more frightening, however, the "show" at the Adams turns history into a special, insider joke. Of course, the kids at a suburban mall might just as easily laugh at the stupidity of *Friday the 13th*, but I suspect that there anxiety is more often the source of humor. And in any case, the kids—and the audience is usually *just* that—are merely outsiders. Downtown, the dramatization of dismemberment represents a kind of symbolic, group autobiography. And it still becomes the subject of joking, the centerpiece of a communal circus for everybody who's left here after history has happened to them: old people, kids, teenagers, families.

## VI: Being Correct

This brings up the question of my own participation and the possibility that what I see going on at the movies is as much a projection of my own as the diagnosed condition of postmodernism. To make a long story short, I am an "urban pioneer"—so much so, in fact, that I moved into my apartment near the Park before the term "Yuppie" had even been invented. I arrived in Detroit on the very day that Dayton-Hudson announced the closing of their great downtown store. My address could be interpreted in any number of different ways, then, ranging from politically correct, to courageous, to confused. Whatever the verdict, I am a typical subject, critically. Downtown is "coming back," and I am the result, a suburban arriviste. Similarly, history is coming back in the post-historical discourse that I have tried to write myself into here, again typically, though I hope as somewhat less of an arriviste.

What I value about this written-over place I have come to live in is not my being a part of it, but my being able to watch it from outside; I live near the Park, but historically speaking, there's no way for me to get there from here, nor do I want to. Neither do I wish it to change, in some ways, though I recognize that the very fact of my being here has already made things different. But so long as difference gets taken seriously, it may still become the basis of intelligence:

> Finally, it must be clear that it is our business not to supply reality but to invent allusions to the conceivable which cannot be presented. . . . The nineteenth and twentieth centuries have given us as much terror as we can take. We have paid a high enough price for the nostalgia of the whole and the one, for the reconciliation of the concept and the sensible, of the transparent and the communicable experience. Under the general demand for slackening and for appeasement, we can hear the mutterings of the desire for a return of terror, for the realization of the fantasy to seize reality. The answer is: Let us wage a war on totality; let us be witnesses to the unpresentable; let us activate the differences and save the honor of the name. (81–82)

That's the way Jean-François Lyotard ends his study, *The Post-Modern Condition*, and it strikes me as a hopeful conclusion, though perhaps no less ambiguously so than the postmodern conclusion of Detroit itself. From both inside and outside, people project terror—staged as well as real—onto this place in order to totalize it, whether destructively or constructively, whether in the name of removal or of renewal, although it's often hard to tell the difference. In either case, what stands to be lost is more than the bunk of history, which has been of questionable value, at least since Henry Ford. What stands to be lost is all the time it took to see through Detroit and what this city represents (for good and ill)—a seeing through that has been conducted more effectively and painfully here, perhaps, than anywhere else. To that end, there is no place better for intelligence than the old theaters on the Park, which remain at the center of this post-historical town. But it remains to be seen how much longer such places will last and how much longer the differences they represent will remain intelligible, particularly if more people like me continue to show up downtown.

## VII: Epilogue

As to how much longer the old downtown theaters would last, the answer was not very long. All of them are gone now, one way or another. The Adams closed permanently after a shooting at the opening of Run DMC's movie, *Tougher Than Leather.* By that time, the Madison had been out of business for a year or more. The Plaza went under too and then came back as a not-very-successful art house, before its new owner finally gave up. Now it's a sometimes venue for "Apollo-style" talent shows. The State never resumed its role as a movie theater; first a Chicago entrepreneur leased it and turned it into ClubLand ("the greatest party in the free world"); when he decamped, the owner copied that idea with his own Club X, which is holding its own with a mostly white, suburban crowd. Next door, the Fox has become the object of a costly restoration and now hosts expensive road shows and theatrical productions, and maybe twice a year, a classic nostalgia film. (*Casablanca* played a while back; *The Wizard of Oz* is on now.) Developers, encouraged by the success of the Fox in particular, have bought all the old palaces, each of which is now subject to one renewal plan or another. None of them is slated to become a neighborhood theater again.

# Renewal

## The Humiliation of History

*[Detroit] . . . a city that throws a shadow over tomorrow.*
—CNN, 20 September 1992

### I: At the Bar

It was impossible to hear what he had said—the aging black man, sitting on the barstool next to mine, at the Elwood, which had only been open for a couple of weeks. At least that's how long it had been open *this* time around. For fifty years, starting in 1936, the Elwood Bar and Grill had served food and drinks at the same corner on Woodward, across from the Fox and the State theaters, and just a couple of blocks away from the hotels and office towers built around the Grand Circus Park in the years right before the First World War, back when this was the center of downtown. But by the mid-1980s, both theaters had closed; the hotels were gutted, abandoned hulks; and the office towers stood deserted, like most of the retail space on Woodward; the tenants had long since moved to either the suburbs or newer addresses at the Renaissance Center, or maybe further out along the Detroit River. So the Elwood closed too.

When I glance up into the mirror behind the bar, I find myself staring into the old man's face, reflected there. He nods and raises his small glass of beer in a toast, but he doesn't drink any. The bar we're both leaning on was probably topped with zinc, originally. The surface now is thinly cut agate; there are fluorescent tubes beneath, and when their illumination passes through the translucent stone, it gives everyone an odd look, like when you were kids and you shined a flashlight up from under your chin at a slumber party to creep out your friends. The way my face looks now, in the mirror, is like that, or—it occurs to me—really more like the scene from *The Shining* when Jack Nicholson sits in that eerie bar, in the deserted hotel, sharing a cocktail with the ghosts. I raise my martini glass and smile back at the man in the mirror.

He tries to scoot his stool closer to mine, so he'll have a better chance at making himself heard, though the odds are not good. The noise level in here is pretty high, which is obviously how the designer planned things. Floors, walls, and ceilings are all hard surfaced, so that even if the place was half empty (which it isn't tonight) the echo would still make it sound like there's a real party going on. "This Art Deco style diner was built in 1936 . . . as a neighborhood bar and grill to service the Theatre District and office clientele of Grand Circus Park," a little brochure will inform curious visitors: "[the Elwood] was transformed in 1988 by owner Chuck Forbes into a glittering nightspot to service the 'new' clientele of the restored district. This architectural gem is listed on the National Register of Historic Places. Its compact design suggests the coming of 'streamline' Art Moderne styling." The man tries once more to make himself heard. I strain to understand what he is saying over the noise of other conversations, the banging of dishes and silver, the shouted orders of the mostly college-kid staff, who are gotten up to look like carhops from some postmodern Archie comic. And there's the jukebox too, a big restoration Wurlitzer; it's been playing Glenn Miller records nonstop.

Finally "Chattanooga Choo-Choo" finishes, and I'm able to make out what the man has been trying to tell me. "This is our place," he says, smiling, raising his glass again, and this time taking a sip of beer. "Our place," he repeats, and nods toward the woman sitting on the stool next to his. She is his age; she's wearing a little cloche hat with rhinestones on it, and a short veil. She holds a crutch under her arm. That's all the man wanted to say, apparently. He and the woman, who I expect must be his wife, sit there looking around the room, smiling, holding onto their two small glasses of beer, which they have hardly drunk any of. They seem glad to be back in "their place," now that it's open again, although it's obvious their lease has already expired.

You don't have to read the pamphlet to know the Elwood doesn't really belong to the old man. Chuck Forbes, the actual owner, is a locally famous success story—sort of. He left his job with Ford Motor Company and started buying downtown real estate back when nobody else wanted it. For a long time, people mostly thought he was crazy; and a lot of them probably still do, which is why Forbes's success is only a "sort of" proposition. He's saved some fine pieces of architecture, like the Elwood, but it remains to be seen whether his investment will pay off. Which is something the old man probably understands. He looks of an age that he could have come to the Elwood's first opening fifty years ago, although he might not have been welcome back then. The bar didn't really get to be his until the people who built downtown quit wanting it. That's when the old man and his wife inherited the city —this part of it, at least—by default. And maybe they'll get it back again. Historically speaking, it's belonged to them for a lot longer, now, than it has to the people—mostly white, middle-class, and suburban—who are standing three deep at the bar and waiting out on the sidewalk to get in.

The city for them has become a purely recreational destination: one that is superfluous to the necessities of housing, shopping, or work. The middle class no longer depends on cities as it did a hundred years ago, or even thirty years ago, when per capita income was still 5 percent higher in town than in the suburbs. Today, only about a quarter of the population live in central cities, and their income, which is 59 percent lower than suburbia, is a clear indication of who got left behind: the old, the poor, the sick (Lacayo 31). This new demographic fact of life has led Joel Garreau to propose the term "edge city" to describe the urban configurations, which as he puts it, are not "sub" anything, but define a free-standing category all on their own:

> Edge Cities represent the third wave of our lives pushing into new frontiers in this half century. First, we moved our homes out past the traditional idea of what constituted a city. . . . Then we wearied of returning downtown for the necessities of life, so we moved our marketplaces out to where we lived. . . . Today, we have moved our means of creating wealth, the essence of urbanism—our jobs—out to where most of us have lived and shopped for two generations. That has led to the rise of Edge City. (4)

By Garreau's reckoning, that's the place most Americans now call home; it surely represents the kind of existence the majority of the middle class imagine when they think of the Good Life. And regardless of economic facts to the contrary, more than 90 percent of Americans continue to identify themselves as middle class (Samuelson 34), which means that for most of us, the old centered city is in every sense outmoded: it's not where we dwell any longer, in either fact or in imagination.

Nevertheless, for reasons of both sentiment and practicality, certain civic institutions remain where they always have, with Detroit being typical. Downtown is still where people have to come for the Symphony, the Institute of Arts, and the Michigan Opera Theater; it's where the Tigers play baseball and the Red Wings play hockey; it's also home to the city and county jails and the courts. (Football has long since moved to the "edge," along with basketball.) Bank headquarters remain downtown, along with accountants' offices and large law firms—the kinds of operations where people benefit by being close enough to each other so they can do business face to face. Generally, such concerns are found in large, high-rise towers, with the basically stable (and self-contained) population of workers moving from older places to newer ones, as buildings open up. For most people, though, most of the time, the once unavoidable city has become a sometimes proposition. There's nothing left that would preserve the day-to-day relevance of downtown—with a single, paradoxical exception.

For both good and ill, the city has one resource that suburbs and edge cities don't: it has a past. The same thing that drove people out of town—their sense of what history has made of urban life—is also what brings them back. But with a difference. The family that moved out of the old neighborhood in the 1950s or 1960s is probably not going to want to go back there. And those people long since quit coming in to movies and stores and restaurants, so that most of the establishments that defined a quotidian civic culture twenty or thirty or forty years ago have gone out of business, or else followed their clients into suburban reinvention. This is not always the case, of course. One or two exceptions exist, in addition to the institutional hold-outs. The pleasantest in Detroit, surely, is the Caucus Club, which is not really a club, although it was gotten up to look like one, or like one might have appeared in 1952 when the place first opened to great success on the ground floor of the city's (then) tallest building, with its dark paneling, brass sconces, and a group of employees that could only be described as a staff. (This was the time when downtown businesses did the highest dollar volume they ever had, or would.) Until the mid-1980s, you could still walk into the place, at 10:00 or 11:00 at night. "Dinner this evening, or just drinks?" you would be asked by the hostess with the changeless 1950s hairstyle, wearing the nice little cocktail dress. And you could sit, over steaks or Dover sole, and listen to the singer and her accompanist: you and the owner, who would possibly be the only other person in the dining room. These days, the singer and piano player are gone, along with the owner, and so is the hostess with the changeless hair; and the Caucus Club closes by 8:00 each night because when people come back downtown, it's not places like this that they want to come back to.

The Caucus Club is too implicated, historically, to be inviting; it reminds people of the city they once lived in and still remember (and decided to leave): a city uncomfortably familiar in its humiliation and therefore no fit subject for speculation. The places that succeed, nowadays, have nothing to do with that city. Instead, they invite patrons into a past that is beguiling precisely because it is not historical in any practical sense. This elective past—unlike the past of institutional hold-outs or the posthumous Caucus Club—lies just beyond the precincts of living memory; it defines a kind of "edge" history, of which the Elwood is typical. The crowds that have made the place a success are nostalgically motivated, just like the old man and his wife. They have each been separated, temporally, from their object of desire, which is the basis of all nostalgias. But that's where the similarity ends. The history that brought the old man to the Elwood and made it his place is what has been effaced in order "to service the 'new' clientele of the restored district," none of whom had probably set foot in this bar until after it first closed and then reopened. The "restoration" of their putative past brings them—brings me—here and also places his historical tenancy in jeopardy.

Strictly speaking, this is no restoration at all, then. There is no attempt to return the Elwood to some former state: as it might have appeared on opening day in 1936, for example; or in the 1940s, when Glenn Miller's music was popular; or in the 1950s, when the Wurlitzer was new and the car-hop uniforms were current; or in the 1970s or early 1980s, when the old man might have sat here at the bar having a beer, one of the solitary drinkers I used to glimpse through the grimy window as I rode by on the Woodward bus. The restoration undertaken so successfully here is one that humiliates history of its narrative authority to separate one moment from the next, so that the past becomes a jumble of period styles and details: some of them "authentic," like the exterior of the building itself; others reproductions, like the car-hop uniforms and the deco fittings; still others purely synthetic, like the agate-topped bar and the high-gloss woodwork.

This is no botched job, however; the anachronism is self-conscious, intentional, and beautifully executed. At the same time, it would be a mistake to construe this project as a postmodern "pastiche," the term Fredric Jameson applies to denote the opposite of "real history": "the complacent eclecticism . . . which randomly and without principle but with gusto cannibalizes all the architectural styles of the past and combines them in overstimulating ensembles" (1991: 18–19). This is precisely *not* how the Elwood is perceived—as a construction that is complacent, eclectic, random, a cannibalizing of style. The project becomes intelligible, and desirable, as something at once new, but at the same time, historically genuine. "How sweet it is," *Detroit Monthly* enthuses in its restaurant listing, four years after the reopening of the Elwood: "to see this terrific renovation of Detroit period architecture across the street from the refurbished Fox Theatre. The exterior remains much as it was, but look inside for a sleek new look and a lovely bar" ("Restaurants" 70). It is the conflation of history and news—a "sleek new look"—or rather the rendering of history as news that makes the Elwood a success: "a smashingly smart Art Deco watering hole, a big hit with Yuppies after work," as the *Hunts' Guide to Southeast Michigan* advises prospective tourists (Hunt 41).

The past provides the city with an intelligibility that history, unaided—*unrestored*—remains incapable of, particularly for the middle-class, "Yuppie" clientele, who now discovers a positive need to come back downtown from the ex-urban "edge" where professionals mostly work and live. As the *Hunts' Guide* suggests, this formerly abandoned place—part of it at least—becomes necessary to the conduct of a "smart" life(style). And the difference, perhaps—between an obfuscatory *then* and a standing-room-only *now*—is intention. The past that makes the Elwood desirable (and that will soon displace the old man and his wife) is all invented: not history, but something constructed out of it. The music, the uniforms, the exterior design of the Elwood, which "suggests the coming of 'streamline' Art Moderne styling," the interior fittings—the Wurlitzer, the bar, the imitation/retro neon clock—all invite inquiry; each detail induces a certain "nostalgia for the present," as Jameson has called it: "It can first and foremost be defined as a perception of the present as history: that is, as a relationship to the present which somehow defamiliarizes it and allows us that distance from immediacy which we call historical" (1989: 523). But this nostalgic distancing doesn't go unrequited, as Jameson supposes; on the contrary, it invites an inquiry that the hyper-stylization of this space at once satisfies as consumable and self-locating intelligence. Each anachronistic detail appeals to an explanation, which cancels the freehold of the old man, whose only competence is memory, and invites the conservancy of a class able to recognize the relevance of information: information about the provenance of objects, the genealogy of old songs, the origin of architectural styles. The point, in other words, is not the restoration *of* history, but restoration *as* the presumptive history of a "new" proprietorship.

This same economy of desire and self-recognition becomes even more visible—literally—across the street at a second new/old establishment called Tres Vite, which, together with the Elwood, makes a little textbook study in the varieties of urban renewal: one based on restoration, the other on conversion; and both crucially economized by information. Tres Vite occupies the corner space of the old Fox Theater Building, where Henry the Hatter (once among Detroit's most prestigious haberdashers) had his downtown store. As an example of successful renewal, this restaurant exemplifies the inside-out strategy on which conversions are typically founded. Walls that were once opaque are now made of glass, so that among the most private of public acts—up-scale dining—is turned into a streetside spectacle, with patrons being separated from pedestrians by only a quarter inch of transparency. What is more, the conversion of the space itself has become an extension of the specular inquiry to which diners are submitted. Walls and ceiling are intentionally "distressed"; there are holes in the plaster where fixtures and fittings have been stripped away in a studied, haphazard fashion. The point is not to appear finished (in the sense of a now irrelevant and abandoned history), but to be *visibly* in conversion, which is why the walls have all been turned transparent: in order to make clear what is going on.

Not just visibility is at stake, though. There are coffee shops and diners all over town where people can sit by windows, seeing and being seen. Something more is under way; it involves not only the designer space, with its signature furniture and expensive appointments, but also the conversion of diners themselves. The individual here submits to a desirable interrogation, or rather to an interrogation that demonstrates a convert's desire. "Chic rules," according to

*Detroit Monthly*, "whether in the menu . . . or in the striking appointments and design-conscious clientele" ("Restaurants" 77). The politics of chic begin at the front doors, which enforce a timely nostalgia for missing information. The doors are right where they always were, along both exterior walls, except that none of them is functional. The uninitiated frequently humiliate themselves visibly in their attempts to discover the secret of entry. They try first one, then another, making their way helplessly along the glass walls, a comic diversion for diners and pedestrians alike. The real door is located in an interior arcade; and it too plays a little joke on clients, as if to offer a final reminder of the humiliations that lie ahead. "Push" is what the lettering on the beautifully restored brass and mahogany frame reads, but you can only open the door by pulling. And by the time you figure that out, the hostess—dressed in redoubtable black, with expensive heels and henna hair and the stylish pallor of haute couture—will have begun making signs, through the window, as if trying to communicate with a simpleton, or a child.

This might make it seem that the place would be unpopular. But just the reverse is true. People, lots of them, come to Tres Vite—just as they come to the Elwood—because they need to: they find something here that they can't get anywhere else; they want to submit to an inquiry that will lead them, sooner or later, to the discovery of "new" rights: rights that will entitle them to deface historic structures in the name of conservancy, that will enable an informational foreclosure on the old man, who is in no position to understand the bar he has presumptuously called his own.

In an apt, and much reproduced, phrase, Guy Debord has referred to our present media culture as a "society of the spectacle," by which he means a society organized by a phantasmagoria of images that takes the place of history:

> Another side of the deficiency of general historical life is that individual life as yet has no history. The pseudo-events which rush by in spectacular dramatizations have not been lived by those informed of them; moreover they are lost in the inflation of their hurried replacement at every throb of the spectacular machinery. . . .

> This individual experience of separate daily life remains without language, without concept, without critical access to its own past which has been recorded nowhere. (no. 157)

That would be true, of course, except for the project of posturban renewal. Tres Vite, for example, finds its success precisely in opposition to this state of simulacral by-standing. To be under interrogation there is to escape the aphasic isolation of Debord's spectacular subject, who is the subject—theoretically and critically—of the postmodern project(ion) generally.

It is not to preserve history but to humiliate it that Tres Vite and the Elwood are in business. But that humiliation—when repeated—*becomes* a kind of history, which is both democratic and also a little mean. Not merely with the joke of the false front doors and the superior hostess, but with the food and service as well. The menu, like the clothes people wear here, is "unconstructed," which is to say, the historically constituted categories that inform middle-class taste have been visibly dissolved. The narrative of courses gives way to an informational simultaneity, so that sandwiches and pizza and pasta and main dishes are mixed indifferently together: on the dinner menu for March 30 at Tres Vite, for instance, "scallop ravioli with capers, saffron cream and basil" appears with the "club sandwich," which appears with the "tomato, caper and basil pizza." Ordering places the individual diner in a position of special exposure vis-à-vis the serviceable interrogation of the thoroughly deconstructed "waitstaff," who in their hip appropriation of traditional regalia (white jackets, napkins over the arm, crumb brushes after dinner—combined with tattoos, unisex ear studs, and designer hair) humiliate the very proprieties on which history—as the exclusionary practice of bourgeois culture—is based. And that is the point.

Tres Vite translates suburban isolation—"without language, without concept, without critical access to its own past"—into an on-screen performance: a kind of Oprah Moment. Oprah's clients, like the clients at Tres Vite, are communicants of a simple truth; namely, that a life in conversion is not subject to the old narrative rules of order: the culture of waiting, saving, amounting to something. To be in conversion *is* a life; it *is* a history that allows the otherwise uninformed subject to testify and, what is more, to assume the presumptive right of a convert's new-born virtue. This makes Tres Vite, with its "very quick" fix on subjectivity, quite different from the restaurants it has supplanted—the Caucus Club, for instance, or the even more exclusive London Chop House. There the politics of arrival were practiced with a scrupulous, time-honoring care. Those places were dark, private, sequestered from the common view; they were founded on a cultural opacity that information has now all but seen through (with the Caucus Club retaining only a vestigial, lunch-time clientele, and the Chop House having gone bankrupt several years ago). The conservation of status, like the conservation of the currency, was based on hoarding; the best tables (booth one or two, at the Chop House) were reserved for the patrons who had earned them. By contrast, there *is* no best table at Tres Vite, where the therapeutics of conversion are practiced with a Jacobin, democratic zeal. "Patrons," whose practice of sociality is now largely conducted in private, rarely come to such unfamiliar places, where attitude displaces identity, where the momentary economy of information defines the basis of all transactions.

This returns things, in a way, to the old man, who sits benignly on his stool, nodding around the room, as if welcoming this unexpected crowd to his place. The weird light from the bar seems just right for our spectral interview: he's a displaced spirit from a past that is gone; I'm from one that never existed. And we've come together here, two ghosts to haunt each other's reflections—mine, I expect, more than his. It's clear we'll never drink together again.

## II: William Dean Howells Among the Chinese

In *Sister Carrie*, Theodore Dreiser imagines a place—a restaurant called Rector's—that functions very much as the Caucus Club or the Chop House used to. It's there that he sends his traveling salesman Eddie Drouet to indulge in the ceremony of commercial self-recognitions on which the city—*that* city of centered representations—was founded:

> He only craved the best, as his mind conceived it, and such doings seemed to him a part of the best. Rector's, with its polished marble walls and floor, its profusion of lights, its show of china and silverware, and, above all, its reputation as a resort for actors and professional men, seemed to him the proper place for a successful man to go. . . . When dining, it was a source of keen satisfaction to him to know that Joseph Jefferson was wont to come to this same place, or that Henry E. Dixey, a well-known performer of the day, was then only a few tables off. At Rector's he could always obtain this satisfaction, for there one could encounter politicians, brokers, actors, some rich young "rounders" of the town, all eating and drinking amid a buzz of popular commonplace conversation. (44)

Such representational institutions, or rather the institutionalized representation they stand for, make Dreiser's fictional typology possible. He has a convert's faith in metropolitan intelligence, which finds expression in his novelistic omniscience generally, and in particular, in the city as both its instrument and origin. "It must be," Dreiser writes, in describing Fitzgerald and Moy's elegant saloon, to which Druet goes for an after-dinner drink, "that a strange bundle of passions and vague desires give rise to such a curious social institution or it would not be" (48). That the institution exists, as a subject for novelistic curiosity, is what makes the frequenters of it intelligible and Dreiser's insights possible.

As the level of self-consciousness evident in his description implies, the "reality" on which literary realism was founded could not be assumed as a given; instead, it was a special effect created by a convergence of talent and need. The institutional omniscience of the city, which achieves artistic expression in the realist novel, offered a necessary reassurance in the face of creeping relativism: the suspicion that the truth of urban culture was merely a by-product of commercial exploitation and therefore liable to humiliation. In *A Modern Instance* (1882), William Dean Howells both invokes this suspicion and ironically anneals it in a passage describing the town house where the parents of one of his main characters, Ben Halleck, live:

> As for the interior of the house, it had been furnished, once for all, in the worst style of that most tasteless period of household art which prevailed from 1840 to 1870; and it would be impossible to say which was most hideous, the carpets or the chandeliers, the curtains or the chairs and sofas; crude colors, lumpish and meaningless forms, abounded in a rich and horrible discord. The old people thought it all beautiful, and those daughters who had come into the new house as little girls revered it; but Ben and his youngest sister, who had been born in the house, used the right of children of their parents' declining years to laugh at it. Yet they laughed with a sort of filial tenderness. (1977: 205)

The fault of the old people is one of historic misapprehension; they form a sentimental attachment to the material signified of culture and fail, consequently, to apprehend the "reality" of their situation, which is vouchsafed to the younger children and through them, ironically, to the reader as well. For a class who had taken up residence at the precise vanishing point of history, and whose existence depended on maintaining that problematic address, the refusal to understand life *as* on-going representation—while comic here—elsewhere takes on a high moral seriousness.

In 1890, with *A Hazard of New Fortunes*, Howells brought two of his most popular characters—Basil and Isabel March, the couple originated in *Their Wedding Journey*—from Boston, the capital of culture, to New York, the emerging capital of commerce. (Howells would soon undertake the same move himself.) This fictional contingency allowed him access to the city as a distinctly "modern" problem—a problem that at once calls into question the history his protagonists embody:

> The whole at moments seemed [to March] lawless, Godless; the absence of intelligent, comprehensive purpose in the huge disorder, and the violent struggle to subordinate the result to the greater

> good, penetrated with its dumb appeal the consciousness of a man who had always been too self-enwrapt to perceive the chaos to which the individual selfishness must always lead. But there was still nothing definite, nothing better than a vague discomfort, however poignant, in his half recognition of such facts. . . . (1976: 184)

The knowing humiliation of this character's sensibility and point of view is what specifically valorizes the authority, and irony, of the novel's omniscient, narratorial representations.

In the same passage, Howells sends March on a walk through lower Manhattan to Mott Street in Chinatown, where Basil registers directly the problematic humbling of his middle-class presumptions:

> It seemed for some reason to be a day of leisure with the Chinese dwellers of Mott Street. . . . They stood about the tops of basement stairs, and walked two and two along the dirty pavement, with their little hands tucked into their sleeves across their breasts, aloof in immaculate cleanliness from the filth around them, and scrutinizing the scene with that cynical sneer of faint surprise to which all aspects of our civilization seem to move their superiority. Their numbers gave ethnical character to the street, and rendered not them, but what was foreign to them, strange there; so that March had a sense of missionary quality in the old Catholic church, built long before their incursion was dreamt of. It seemed to have come to them there, and he fancied in the statued saint that looked down from its facade something not so much tolerant as tolerated, something propitiatory, almost deprecative. (1976: 185–86)

The passage ends with March's being distracted from these reflections by the arrival of the police, who are bringing home a drunk woman: "Presently a Christian mother appeared, pushed along by two policemen on a handcart, with a gelatinous tremor over the paving and a gelatinous jouncing at the curb-stones"(1976: 186). The neighborhood children interrupt their play and follow along after the woman. And it's then that March finally understands the city, which had appeared only just earlier to be lawless and without intelligence:

> March understood the unwillingness of the poor to leave the worst conditions in the city for comfort and plenty in the country when he reflected upon this dramatic incident, one of many no doubt which daily occur to entertain them in such streets. A small town could rarely offer anything comparable to it, and the country never. He said that if life appeared so hopeless to him as it must to the dwellers in that neighborhood he should not himself be willing to quit its distractions, its alleviations, for the vague promise of unknown good in the distance somewhere. (1976: 186)

The passage, like the novel as a whole, is worth spending time on because it illustrates—in one of the most successful works of a popularly "serious" author—the precise convergence of humiliations that defines the history of middle-class culture: on the one hand, the desire Basil feels to repudiate the past and join other "self-made" men in New York; on the other, the anxiety that overtakes him when he does.

March's cultivated presumptions are clearly humiliated by the city, which appears to him "lawless, Godless; the absence of intelligent, comprehensive purpose." The historical authority of culture, which he represents, is here dissipated and valueless, so that the emblematic Christian saint figures his own position, "not so much tolerant as tolerated, something propitiatory, almost deprecative." Basil's putative insights are no more reliable than those of the neighborhood rabble, who are pleasantly distracted—as he is—by the comic spectacle of the drunk woman being wheeled home by the police. The city, which is called into being by a wishful humiliation of history (such as takes place in the self-satisfied assessment of the Halleck interior), is knowable on precisely those terms: as an ongoing convergence of humiliations; that *is* its truth, its "reality." One thing, of course, is not subject to humiliation, and that is representation itself. The more frequently (and recognizably) individuals such as Basil falter before the enormity of urban experience, the greater the power of Howells' authorial representations of that experience; they take the place of a "comprehensive purpose in the huge disorder," and in this his realism consists. Increasingly, middle-class culture would be driven by and toward representation itself as a substitute for understanding, in politics, the arts, and commercial advertising, so that Howells' problematizing, ironic commentary becomes continuous with truth, or rather with the absence of truth, which his novels compensate mimetically, "realistically."

His reading, which turns historical conundrum into an ironically settled question of representation, remains current and popular, long after first apprehension, from Fitzgerald to Lewis and beyond, ending up with *Goodbye Columbus* (1959), where Philip Roth contemplates through a first-person narrator the depopulation of the city and with it, the final exhaustion of history:

> The old Jews like my grandparents had struggled and died, and their offspring had struggled and prospered, and moved further and further west towards the edge of Newark, then out of it, and up the slope of the Orange Mountains, until they had reached the crest and started down the other side, pouring into Gentile territory as the Scotch-Irish had poured through the Cumberland Gap. Now, in fact, the Negroes were making the same migration. . . . Who would come after the Negroes? Who was left? No one, I thought, and someday these streets, where my grandmother drank hot tea from an old *jahrzeit* glass would be empty and we would all of us have moved to the crest of the Orange Mountains, and wouldn't the dead stop kicking at the slats in their coffins then? (64–65)

The dream of Roth's narrator is one that comes at the suburbanized end of history, when there will be nothing, and nobody, left to represent in the city, so that "the dead," in that beautiful phrase, are finally able to "stop kicking at the slats in their coffins." At that moment, the realist novel—already confined to a first-person point of view—finally becomes unnecessary because the question of historical representation, to which it is the answer, will likewise cease to have meaning.

This moment of unimaginable quiet has obviously not arrived. The city never went away, any more than the novel did, so it makes no sense to talk about either of them as coming back. The history of both is still under humiliation. What *has* changed in the thirty-odd years since *Goodbye Columbus* was written is the terms of middle-class habitation and now reinhabitation. The middle class whom history finally divested of their presumptive lease on omniscience are not the same people who return to the city, or to the novel, as if nothing had happened. Which leads to the peculiar, if illustrative, episode of Tom Wolfe and *The Bonfire of the Vanities.* He wrote the novel serially and rather unsuccessfully for *Rolling Stone* and then issued a much revised and amplified version in book form in October 1987. Two years later, in the winter of 1989, a gossip-induced (and soon-to-be-unsuccessful) movie version of the novel was in production, and Wolfe published a long essay ("a literary manifesto for the new social novel") in *Harper's* magazine where he made an ardent plea for the renewal of realist fiction: "At this weak, pale, tabescent moment in the history of American literature, we need a battalion, a brigade, of Zolas to head out into this wild, bizarre, unpredictable, Hog-stomping Baroque country of ours and reclaim it as literary property" (1989: 55). As Wolfe makes clear in the little autobiographical bildungsroman that informs his essay, he has taken his own advice and rediscovered the present as historical and historically relevant in precisely the terms recorded in the realist novel.

Two things are instructive about this case: first is Wolfe's apparent and much criticized ignorance of writers who seemed to be doing just what he alone claimed to have undertaken; second, and far more interesting, is his illustrative misapprehension of his own novel, which he apparently thought was equivalent to, and continuous with the work of Dickens, Thackeray, and Zola. As to the first point, many people—many of them writers—hurried into print to assure Wolfe that if he only read more books, he would not have had to despair of the novel. "The overwhelming impression one gets," as Robert Towers pointed out in the *New York Times Book Review*, "is that Mr. Wolfe has read very little of the fiction of the last 30 years" (15). Towers then goes on to note novelists who appear to be writing precisely the kinds of books Tom Wolfe so desperately, if disingenuously, deplores the lack of.

As to the second, more interesting point, Wolfe demonstrates with special clarity the misrecognition that sustains renewal projects, novelistic or otherwise. Renewal is always personal, an affair of self-discovery, so that the returnee has to believe he is the first, or near the first, to catch on. This is why everybody at Tres Vite, for example, is made to feel like an outsider because the trick is to convert history into relevant news; and the news—like any other form of information—is only valuable so long as it is fresh, which is to say, only so long as *everybody else* doesn't know it. So, Wolfe had to be the first to renew the novelistic purchase on the city, even though it was obvious to everyone—himself included, most likely—that he wasn't. ("Literature" aside, any casual reader must be aware that the city has consistently been a subject of realistic interest, and exploitation, above all to crime writers, from Edgar Allan Poe to Elmore Leonard and Loren Estleman.) "Meantime," he wrote in the *Harper's* article, "I turned to the proposed nonfiction novel about New York. As I saw it, such a book should be a novel *of the city*, in the sense that Balzac and Zola had written novels *of Paris* and Dickens and Thackeray had written novels *of London*, with the city always in the foreground, exerting its relentless pressure on the souls of its inhabitants" (1989: 46). The question is what form this "pressure" takes. In Balzac and Zola and Dickens, the pressure had been obviously narrative in origin: the pressure to make a life, to master the economy of urban culture; learning "how to shop," as Isabel March would later put it. By the time Wolfe wrote *Bonfire*, the pressure was no less "relentless," but its form was wholly different, so that the narrative plotting of his novel, rather than defining its point, culturally or politically, could be arrived at piecemeal, almost as an afterthought.

This is only to say that neither he nor his detractors seem to have noticed that novels of the city, even crime novels, are no longer based on grand, centered narratives, or on the supposedly "Godless," and therefore distressing dissolution of these. In other words, to write like a Zola or a Dickens (or a Howells or a Dreiser) would be to write in a way completely irrelevant to the historical self-recognition of contemporary readers. The life of the middle-class has been so overtaken by other-than-narrative technologies that the renewal of historically significant fiction—like the renewal of historic buildings—is founded on something else. Books that succeed, as the Elwood or Tres Vite succeed, are about space, not time; their fictional economy is based not on production—making a match, making a deal, making a fortune, making a life, making something representative, in other words—but on information. This is true even of successful pulp fiction, which is often only about the names of things: drinks, restaurants, cars, body parts. And Wolfe is too good a reporter not to get the story right, regardless of what he might have thought he was doing. His novel urges one point with relentless, and topical, precision: namely, that identity and status are economized by information: "Campbell was in the first grade at Taliaferro, which as everybody, *tout le monde*, knew, was pronounced Toliver. Each morning the Taliaferro school dispatched its own bus, bus driver, and children's chaperone up Park Avenue. Few, indeed, were the girls at Taliaferro who did not live within walking distance of that bus route" (1987: 48). It is difficult to imagine Howells or Dreiser writing a passage like that. The city for them was a narratively constituted *place*; its anxieties all had to do with representation and the question of what things could, or should, stand for. The anxiety engendered by Wolfe's text is of an entirely different origin and has nothing to do with either narrative or history. The problem for him is always one of information: not what "tout le monde" knows, but what everyone *doesn't* know, and is therefore liable to regard as important, at least for a while, until everybody does, in fact, occupy the *space* of Wolfe's supposedly omniscient reader, at which point his fiction, like yesterday's stock quotations, will cease to matter. Omniscience here does not define a position of desire and power, as it did under representation; on the contrary, it defines the exhaustion, the end, of informational value, which is why Wolfe, as narrator, is always trying to shame his readers—some of them, at least—into the admission of ignorance, especially an ignorance of appropriate designer names.

The distinction between narrative *then* and informational *now* becomes clear—though not necessarily to Wolfe himself—in the internal dialogue of the mayor when he gets heckled at a Harlem town meeting. "It'll be on TV," the mayor thinks to himself,

> The whole city will see it. They'll love it. Harlem rises up! What a show! . . . They'll sit in their co-ops on Park and Fifth and East Seventy-second Street and Sutton Place, and they'll shiver with the violence of it and enjoy the show. Cattle! Birdbrains! Rosebuds! *Goyim*! You don't even know, do you? Do you really think this is *your* city any longer? Open your eyes! The greatest city of the twentieth century! Do you think *money* will keep it yours? Come down from your swell co-ops, you general partners and merger lawyers! It's the Third World down there! (1987: 6–7)

Those partners do come down, of course, but not to the third-world city the mayor imagines; nor do they come down to the old city of narrative contracts and readerly omniscience. They come down instead to a "second city" of informed renewals that money, in fact, *did* build and that money keeps safe (Herron 66).

They come down to a city of present-tense space that exists as an excavation on the history of the old city of narrative production (Jameson 1984: 64): "You are not the kind of guy who would be at a place like this at this time of the morning. But here you are, and you cannot say that the terrain is entirely unfamiliar, although the details are fuzzy" (1). Thus the opening sentences of Jay McInerney's *Bright Lights, Big City*, which—in its drug-induced up/down economy—privileges the same vertical axis suggested by Wolfe's mayor. The first city, the city of narrative horizontals—moving to town, getting ahead—is superseded here by a second city: a city of vertical simultaneity. It's the city of Wolfe's co-op towers, the up-time city of McInerney's perpetual present tense. The past is still important, in this city of postnarrative renewal, but not as history; instead, the past invites the forms of conversion and viral coverage that take the place of history, so that Wolfe is exactly right in misrecognizing his own novel as historical and comparing it with Dickens and Zola. He *is* doing just what they were doing; he's writing a history. But the terms, now, are entirely different and unhistorical.

Consider McInerney's self-regarding *you*: "You are not the kind of guy who would be at a place like this at this time of the morning. But here you are." As the novel tries to develop a traditional history, using flash-backs of the narrator's past, it becomes progressively sentimental, sodden, and anachronistic. It's in the present tense that the inside-out city comes to life; and it comes to life specifically as an interrogation. "You" are always being looked at, addressed by various forms of informational speculation:

> The problem is, for some reason you think you are going to meet the kind of girl who is not the kind of girl who would be at a place like this at this time of the morning. When you meet her you are going to tell her that what you really want is a house in the country with a garden. New York, the club scene, bald women—you're tired of all that. Your presence here is only a matter of conducting an experiment in limits, reminding yourself of what you aren't. (3–4)

Identity is momentary and oppositional, a matter of pure *différance* ("reminding yourself of what you *aren't*"), with the endless deferrals of cocaine being essential to the production of a space where there is no time but the present. Here, the subject is assembled, piecemeal, by the "relentless pressure," as Wolfe called it, of a self-othering gaze: the always already of an informational interrogation that is concurrent with the spectation of Tres Vite and with the culture of urban returns generally. *You* only exist as a site of speculation, and when you are no longer being traded at the various addresses of a culturally constituted desire, you dissipate, "crash," into so many scattered, unintelligible fragments. Whereas the reality of Dreiser's characters consisted in their cumulative opacity—in their adding up to something substantial, something withheld, something interior, even if dishonest—everything here gives way to pure transparence.

The near instantaneous pop celebrity of both the novel, *Bright Lights*, and its author, Jay McInerney, suggests a moment of self-recognition on the part of the class called into being by the renewal of the city, or rather by the part of the old middle class whose identity, and ability to reproduce themselves culturally, depended on the informational excavation of the urban past. A more serious—or in any case, a more suggestive—instance of conversion comes in E. L. Doctorow's *Ragtime.* The vertical descent into the always-present second city is like his descent into the historical space of the novel. His intentional mixing of fact and fiction converts the remembered elements of history into an informational quiz. Which part is truth and which is fiction, and does it make any difference? That's the inquiry, or rather speculation, his fiction induces:

> Back home a momentous change was coming over the United States. There was a new President, William Howard Taft, and he took office weighing three hundred and thirty-two pounds. All over the country men began to look at themselves. They were used to drinking great quantities of beer. They customarily devoured loaves of bread and ate prodigiously of the sausage meats of poured offal that lay on the lunch counters of the saloons. The august Pierpont Morgan would routinely consume seven- and eight-course dinners. He ate breakfasts of steaks and chops, eggs, pancakes, broiled fish, rolls and butter, fresh fruit and cream. The consumption of food was a sacrament of success. A man who carried a great stomach before him was thought to be in his prime. Women went into hospitals to die of burst bladders, collapsed lungs, overtaxed hearts and meningitis of the spine. . . . America was a great farting country. All this began to change when Taft moved into the White House. His accession to the one mythic office in the American imagination weighed everyone down. His great figure immediately expressed the apotheosis of that style of man. Thereafter fashion would go the other way and only poor people would be stout. In this regard, as in most others, Evelyn Nesbit was ahead of her time. Her former chief lover Stanford White had been a fashionably burly man, and her husband Harry K. Thaw though not as large was nevertheless soft and wide, but her new lover, Mother's Younger Brother, was as lean and hard as a young tree. (1976: 69–70)

Doctorow's history is a history under conversion: a conversion to the specular truth of information. And while he writes in the traditional past tense, his novel has the feel of a continual present, a present tense of the eye, in which there will be no cumulatively plotted adding up of meaning.

His project in *Ragtime* is not historical representation, then, but renewal: a converting of the once representative past to the presence of visual information:

> Every season of the year wagons came through the streets and picked up bodies of derelicts. Late at night old ladies in babushkas came to the morgue looking for their husbands and sons. The corpses lay on tables of galvanized iron. From the bottom of each table a drainpipe extended to the floor. Around the rim of the table was a culvert. And into the culvert ran the water sprayed constantly over each body from an overhead faucet. The faces of the dead were upturned into the streams of water that poured over them like the irrepressible mechanism in death of their own tears. But somehow piano lessons began to be heard. People stitched themselves to the flag. (1975: 13–14)

He is writing to cover the end of history, like the end of the era of ragtime, which by the end of his novel has "run out, with the heavy breath of the machine, as if history were no more than a tune on a player piano" (1975: 270). Like the novel as a whole, the passage is one of constant movement; there is no catching up with Doctorow's anxiously scanning eye. His is a convert's past, a past *très vite*: not the conservator's luxuriating time of the novel, but the visual space of a movie. And that's where the novel and the city end up, just as they do in *Ragtime*: at the movies.

## III: Decent People Shouldn't Live Here

"Our streets are overrun," the Ed Koch look-alike mayor complains at the beginning of *Batman* (1989), during what is supposed to be a political kick-off rally for a campaign to clean up fictional Gotham City; "Our public officials are helpless." Then he introduces the new district attorney, who has been elected on a tough, anticrime ticket. "Together," the DA tells the guests at the mayor's dinner and also the audience watching on TV, "we can make this city safe for decent people." Jack Nicholson's character—not yet transformed into the Joker—sits on a beautiful leather sofa, in an elegant Gotham duplex, watching the proceedings. "Decent people shouldn't live here," he sneers at the screen and his illicit girlfriend, played by Jerry Hall, "They'd be happier someplace else." But by the end of Reagan's 1980s, when *Batman* was released, the city was clearly a place where decent people wanted to live—lots of them—in just the sort of vertical compounds that Wolfe imagines for his "masters of the universe" and from which Nicholson watches the evening news. The question, then, is on what terms a city which is "overrun" becomes simultaneously a desirable residence; and not merely in fiction, but in fact.

Writing at the time of *Batman*'s release, Paul Goldberger, the architecture critic for the *New York Times*, posed something like the same question; he, along with Tom Wolfe, lamented the lack of appropriate, urban coverage, though in somewhat different terms. "The illness that afflicts the cityspace," he said,

> is not only a matter of human suffering. In a much broader sense, the city is only rarely these days a place of hope, of promise and glory. It is not merely that it is harsh and dirty, for New York and most other American cities have always been harsh and dirty. It is that it has become so indifferent to the very idea of the public realm, to the notion that the city is a collective, shared place, a place that is in the most literal sense common ground. . . . If there is any legacy of the Reagan years, it is to have devalued completely the importance of the public realm and to have raised dramatically the value we place on the private realm, so much so that the public realm has almost ceased to have meaning. (2.1)

The city appears to mock, like Nicholson's character, the very idea of "togetherness," of a "public realm." It's not that things are dirty, or violent—"harsh" per Goldberger's euphemism—because cities have always been that way. What's different is that urban institutions no longer define any "common ground"—at least not one that decent people would consider safe enough to visit—with the result that it has become impossible for citizens to imagine their place in the city as anything other than a necessarily private affair. The city, as collective, middle-class project, consequently appears unrepresentable precisely because it no longer exists, whether politically or artistically, whether for architects and urban planners or for fiction writers; thus the scarcity—in Wolfe's terms—of novels that would record it as other than what it now too obviously has become.

Goldberger is an architect, so it is not surprising that his critique should be fixed in material reality or that he should fail to notice the very development he despairs of. (Wolfe's excuse is more obscure.) As it happens, the city is a subject of intense, imaginative speculation, of precisely the kind that would imply a widespread desire for "common ground," and not just at such narrowly specialized, and infrequent, sites as the Elwood or Tres Vite, or in the postmodern meditations of Paul Auster, say, or Donald Barthelme. But this speculation takes an other-than-architectural (or "writerly") form, or rather, its architecture is not of the sort that results in real estate. The common spaces of the city—now—are mostly to be found in movie theaters, with directors and production designers becoming a more potent force in the definition of urban space than authors of whatever kind, whether architects, city planners, or novelists.

People who live according to cities need not necessarily dwell inside them, in other words; this truth gave rise to one of the most curious of urban ceremonies, the "New York" sing-along. For several years running, in bars all over Detroit and other cities I have visited, the crowd would invariably play that redundant song—"New York, New York"—again and again on the jukebox, or tape machines. Everyone would sing along, a little drunk, feeling somehow better about themselves, and for reasons that have to do specifically with what Goldberger found missing in cities today: a sense of common ground. Rather than making people feel sad about where they weren't, singing "New York, New York" made them feel, unexpectedly, more located in the place where they were. This was not true of the movie, *New York, New York* (1977), that the song came from; the film was directed by Martin Scorsese, and written by Earl Mac Rauch, who grew up and went to school with me, in a dry West Texas town about as far from "the city" as it's possible to get and still be in the United States. Both the script and the production design—with its cartoonish two-dimensionality and postmodern troping—were wrong for the purposes of prospective nostalgia.

But maybe that's why Scorsese's New York would launch a song about somewhere and nowhere simultaneously. The song didn't stand for any particular place so much as it came to stand for the fulfillment of a wish to recognize oneself as a virtual, imaginary resident of the city in general. Start singing the news: the news that the city has become available as a form of coverage now freed from historic residency requirements. Woody Allen, by way of contrast, has turned New York into a place of such vivid personal attachments that the city is hard to imagine except as *his*, a point the voice-over in *Manhattan* makes explicit. Allen's films, consequently, have failed to achieve the broad popular audience that other versions of the city have found. They lack the potential for self-recognition that other, more immediately relevant, entertainments have provided.

For example, with *Dirty Harry* (1971), Clint Eastwood began translating the city into a "common ground" of mutual self-recognitions specifically related to a developing info/serv middle class. Manifestly, his films were the perfect vehicles for the various law-and-order revivals that characterized the 1970s and followed the post-Vietnam rollback of "Great Society" entitlements. Our streets were overrun; our public officials were helpless, as the mayor of Gotham would later put it. Or at least that's how things were made to appear. Perpetrators, typically scripted so as to defy justification, were therefore not to be pitied or coddled (despite the misguided and self-serving interference of bureaucratic pencil-pushers, political opportunists, liberals, affirmative action wimps, and women). Harry Callahan—the old fashioned cop with a variety of ever larger guns—saw criminals and perverts for what they were and generally managed to devise a way around officialdom so that the "perps" would get what they deserved. In that sense, the films—and their popularity—seem consistent with the anti-urbanism (and covert racism), for which law-and-order movements offer a convenient political cover.

In the first film (1971) the villain is a crazed psycho sniper who murders random victims with a high-powered rifle. In the second film (*Magnum Force*, 1973), notable for its increased levels of (now justifiable) violence and brutality, Harry tracks evil doers to the police department itself. In *The Enforcer* (1976) his adversary is an underground terrorist organization. In *Sudden Impact* (1983) he investigates the revenge murders carried out by a woman (played by Sondra Locke), who is getting even with a gang of low-life perverts and rapists. The final Harry vehicle, *The Dead Pool* (1988), has Callahan himself becoming the object of a sleazoid hit-squad. In each instance, the film appeals to the sense of powerlessness that characterizes the middle class, for whom the city—with its now impotent and/or corrupt institutions—has come to stand as a dangerous humiliation, rather than a visible reminder of historic achievement and superiority. Harry acts out the rage of that alienated, "silent majority."

In another, and perhaps more important sense, however, the films are not just about getting even. Their popularity derives at least in part from their rendering both vivid and topical a drama of self-recognition that is not anti-urban, but altogether about reclaiming the city as "common space." And in that sense, Harry is not old-fashioned in the least. On the contrary, he is working for the specific economy of renewal privileged by the return of informational citizens to their once and future home. He recuperates a now unavoidable criminality as a hailing device, so that violence, for Harry, doesn't make the city seem frightening; on the contrary, through his negotiation of violence the city once more becomes intelligible. "Go ahead, make my day," he snarls at a would-be felon, daring him to reciprocate the violence that sustains them both (and giving rise to a feel-good phrase that Ronald Reagan would happily adopt as his own). In such scenes, Harry makes it clear that he and the criminals are the only ones who know what they are doing; they are the only ones for whom the city still makes sense. The pleasure of the fantasy, therefore, regardless of how conscious, is bound up with that essential fact of mutual self-recognition and empowerment.

This same economy of recognition achieves a high-gloss look and —crucially—addresses itself specifically to the subject of historical conversion in Roman Polanski's *Chinatown* (1974), where the urban past devolves upon a search after missing information: about real estate, water rights, paternity, sexuality, clothes. But the basis of the fantasy remains unchanged. Cultural entitlement is here renegotiated, nostalgically, in response to a history of urban humiliations and also *as* a humiliation of unconverted historical space. The city, in retrospect, turns out (all along) to have been about the interests of an emergent class whose fortunes, under conversion, are now based on the production and management of information: information that would make modern Los Angeles possible, both as economic fact and cinematic metaphor. Jack Nicholson's old-fashioned "Jake"—to whom audiences are invited, knowingly, to condescend —may think he understands who people are and that he can make claims against them, based on their behavior, narratively, within the historic frame of the film. But these claims are all trivialized—humiliated—by an economy of private access, which, like the doors at Tres Vite, privileges information not subject to narrative exposition. "Forget it, Jake," Nicholson's sidekick advises his obviously baffled friend because that is the only choice left to the unconverted.

This insight, also the insight of the Harry movies, has been extrapolated in various subsequent films, such as *Beverly Hills Cop* (1984), *Lethal Weapon* (1987), *Robocop* (1987), and their sequels. Each time the message is the same: the city belongs to the people (and automata) in a position to recognize it for what it is; and what it is, is a conversion to an informational economy of self-authorizing humiliations. The question of historically derived rights has been superseded by the more pressing matter of recognition. Arnold Schwarzenegger's *The Terminator* (1984) and *Terminator 2: The Judgment Day* (1991) are perhaps the clearest illustrations of this. In the first film, Schwarzenegger is a future-world villain sent back to "terminate" a woman who will become mother to a (one-day) great leader. He is pursued by a good-guy cop sent to stop him. Between them, these two characters make the urban terrain seem understandably, even acceptably, violent, by virtue of the ultimate struggle that pits them against each other and wastes a lot of civilians in the process. The interchangeability of their opposing positions allows Schwarzenegger to return in *Terminator 2* not as villain, but as good guy, as if to underscore the informational basis of the fantasy, which operates at the level of pure difference, where no fixed cultural signified is either looked for or desired.

Not surprisingly, humiliation becomes the overt subject matter of African-American film makers. Spike Lee's *Do the Right Thing* (1989) is based on a confrontation of Italian-Americans, Asian-Americans, and African-Americans, with the latter being subject to an apparent refusal on the part of "white" immigrant society to let them escape the humiliation of race. Mario Van Peebles' *New Jack City* (1991) provides a ghetto version of Reaganomics, with the discovery of crack cocaine becoming a junk-bond analogue. The rapper Ice-T, himself a former desperado, plays a cop whose inside-trader knowledge allows him to triumph over the evil drug pushers. John Singleton's *Boyz N the Hood* (1991) is a more sober, if less popularly successful, consideration of the same subject matter. In each instance there is a refusal—as in the Harry films—of the old Joe Friday, just-the-facts-ma'am version of the "Naked City," with all its myriad stories. There it was the distance between cops and robbers that organized plots and provided the good guys, from Shane to Peter Gun, a meaningful role, as representatives of civic virtue. Here, there is no virtue, no clearly defined "right thing" to be stood for or done; there is only information and the seemingly interchangeable positions where it is traded. This may account for the lackluster performance of films that have tried to redeem the humiliation of history, as if that project were either relevant or believable. John Sayles's *City of Hope* (1991), Steve Martin's *L.A. Story* (1991), and Lawrence Kasdan's *Grand Canyon* (1991) are all intent on making the city seem possible, narratively, as a place where decent people can learn to live, by inventing stories that bring them back together. These films—far more than Tom Wolfe's novel, or the movie made from it—seem to be doing the work of Dickens and Thackeray; and audiences have taken them more or less that way: as outdated, period pieces with anachronistically modern settings.

As the examples of Harry and Jake and various spin-offs suggest, the forms of recognition that prevail in the city-as-movie, which may be the only city left, are based on a kind of double vision: a self/other opposition working just to the extent that it complicates any final resolution. This fact takes on a pop self-consciousness in one of the most commercially successful movies in history, which not incidentally is also a movie with the city as its main character: but a city nothing like the celebrity-driven cartoon of *Dick Tracy.* The movie, of course, is *Batman* (1989). Does Batman figure the city for safety and redemption, or is he a futile graft onto something more elemental and corrupt? The film is intentionally ambiguous about the answer, and this ambiguity is translated into the black and gold logo that became familiar to every living American. It was up on billboards for months, announcing the arrival of the film that has more than lived up to its hype. First in theaters and now on video cassettes, *Batman* has been "making history the world over," as advertisements proudly proclaimed, with the biggest opening weekend in history, and tape rentals that have surpassed even *E.T.* (In the domestic market alone, the film has already grossed a quarter of a billion dollars.) At first glance, however, it is not clear whether the logo represents a black bat against a gold background or whether it offers a view down a dark throat, through the aperture of devouring, golden teeth. According to the artists who updated this design, the figure-ground ambiguity is intentional and surely relevant to the vision of the city the film represents and to the "history" that *Batman* has been making. (The same ambiguity has been repeated in the logo for the sequel, *Batman Returns*, 1992; a cowled silhouette against a white background resolves either into an image of the caped crusader or else a spiky black hole.)

In *Batman*, Gotham becomes the apotheosis of humiliating history. The city—as interpreted by Anton Furst's production designs—appears as a noxious, inexplicable jumble that mocks the very idea of urbanity. And perhaps most important, Gotham is almost entirely unmarked by external signs, much to the dismay of the nameless, middle-class family who open the film by losing their way, and almost losing their lives. "I know where we are," the father proclaims, as he and his wife and son suddenly find themselves lost in their own town and consequently prey to the criminal inhabitants who will authorize the self-othering appearance of Batman. Unlike *Bladerunner*, to which it is frequently—and mistakenly—compared, as a further extrapolation of postmodern city space, *Batman*'s metropolis refuses to give itself up to signing. Gotham mocks the very idea of legibility. In that sense, it represents faithfully the historical city—the city of dirt and darkness and criminality—that an informationally grounded middle class finds, or else expects to find, when it decides to come back downtown. And if *Batman* represents the illegible city of suburban projection, then the history of that city can be grasped only *through* humiliation. To write it out as traditional narrative, to offer it up as a seamless text, open to a centered reading—which is the object of *Bladerunner*'s film noir coding and voice-over narration—is to sponsor a fundamental lie.

*Batman*'s enduring popularity—despite its critical failure and the lack of effective romantic leads—suggests a certain powerful, if uneasy, self-recognition on the part of audiences, who have also made a success out of *Batman Returns*, despite its even poorer prospects, in terms of advance notices and reviewers' ratings. In both instances, but especially with regard to the first film, it seems not to matter that the usually looked-for elements of a box office success are missing: good story, hopeful ending, romance. What matters is that the city itself emerges as the star, so that the usual trappings of dramatic film—character, plot, theme—are reduced to background. In that sense, *Batman* invites a more complex form of self-recognition than the Harry movies and their clones, which in many ways anticipate it; the film opens a more purely semiotic approach to history. Gotham itself is what matters now, specifically a Gotham that foregrounds the visual politics of renewal.

Looked at from the outside, Furst's city has become an architectural picture of Dorian Gray. Grafted onto the face of the skyscrapers and apartment towers is the physical evidence of trickle-down mendacity. The buildings all appear to be factories; they are all marked with the implements of production that were to have made the city a paradise, but which have instead turned it into a polluted pit, filled with the refuse—both industrial and human—that the urban dream never fully comprehended. It is indeed a place where decent people wouldn't want to live, as Jack Nicholson explains. But at the same time, it's exactly the sort of Gotham—viewed as interior space—that is represented in publications like *Architectural Digest* and *W* as the very place where the beneficiaries of Reaganomics *do* live. The interiors, at least the ones that aren't overtly industrial, offer gorgeous evocations of art deco and art moderne, although no design is pure. Styles and periods are jumbled together in a smart, time-humiliating mix that defies historic supervision. The question, then, is whether the outside humiliates the inside, whether the social overwhelms the individual, or is it the other way around? That's the same question raised by the *Batman* logo, and insofar as the film is concerned, it's probably not possible to say which is true. The film delivers, in immediate, visual and auditory experiences, the thematic lesson of urban renewal, as history degenerates to information and representation gives way to endless, if stylish, deferral. And this is undertaken, and received, not as a nostalgic loss, but as commercially relevant news.

## IV: The Ontology of Wounds

Paradoxical as it may appear, the renewal of the city remains impossible except for the representation and reproduction of violence. In the simplest mnemonic sense, a city without violence would be irrelevant because it would appear unreal to the majority of contemporary Americans. But there is more than just verisimilitude involved, as the otherwise unexpected violence of a film like *Batman* might suggest, in which, for example, Nicholson's Joker horribly mutilates the face of his girlfriend, with the explanation that he is "the world's first fully functioning homicidal artist." The apparently gratuitous application of special effects in the representation of graphic bodily violence is not gratuitous at all, as it turns out, but an essential element of recovery, which is at its most fundamental level a recovery of the body. The people who left the city and those who remain inside it, often trapped by violence, are confronted alike with a disembodied culture: one that demonstrably humiliates the body of its former rights. Citizens—both actual and cinematic—are embarked, therefore, on a process of recovery that devolves upon the humiliated body, which becomes the unavoidable subject of renewal under information.

In Detroit, where the population of guns exceeds that of residents, the murder rate is very high, which makes the city more, rather than less, representative, with regard to urban America generally. So representative has the city become, in fact, that regardless of actual numbers, Detroit maintains its purchase on the popular imagination; despite its no longer being the statistical murder capital of the United States (and consequently of the developed world), the city retains a titular hold on that distinction; it is still thought of and written about as if it were. In that connection, one of the most indicative aspects of local violence relates to the murder rate among young people, children sixteen years of age or less. For this group, there is, on average, one shooting every thirty hours. From among the victims, one dies every nine days. That is one shooting every thirty hours; one murder every nine days. On average. Just for the sixteen and under population. The question is what this means. For a young person, who "has his whole life before him," the loss seems particularly acute and dreadful; it is also a powerful indicator of the crisis that overtakes representational culture in the face of a violation that is—in every worst sense of the term—popular.

It is difficult to naturalize such violence, as merely "what is to be expected" in the city because the participants haven't themselves had time to achieve a conventional, adult perspective. Frequently, it's children who murder other children in a fearful literalizing of Peircean, infinite semiosis. In other words, there is no *presence* outside this violent horizon, no *real* being transgressed. Therefore, nothing is lost, in terms of signification, to the economy of this infinitely regressive system; nor is there anything either to mourn or to fear. As Duane, now age seventeen put it: "You just don't care about getting shot or nothing. Out there you got your own world" (Katz 4).

Speaking of the relation between language and the body, Elaine Scarry reaches the following conclusion that I want to apply to violence generally:

> Physical pain is . . . language-destroying. Torture inflicts bodily pain that is itself language-destroying, but torture also mimes (objectifies in the external environment) this language-destroying capacity in its interrogation, the purpose of which is not to elicit needed information but visibly to deconstruct the prisoner's voice. . . . The prolonged interrogation . . . graphically objectifies the step-by-step backward movement along the path by which language comes into being and which is here being reversed or uncreated or deconstructed. (19–20)

The *authentic* subject, in Scarry's terms, is the one who can no longer speak because the body has been deprived of language with which to communicate a situation, an identity. That is what it means to be interrogated. In terms of the violence that characterizes contemporary American society, the very possibility of language is consequently disauthenticating, unreal.

This is particularly true of the language of traditional, middle-class identity: the narrative discourse of which individual lives are constructed. As one Detroit detective said, speaking of the young people who are so often the popular subjects of violence—popular statistically and also in terms of the ideological privileging of violent representations—"These kids have not lived, they have not seen or done anything with their lives. They grow up on the streets, and that is where they die. They go from school to the streets and then to the morgue" (Zeiger, Grant 10A). So successful has their historical interrogation been, in Scarry's terms, that there is no communicable life for them to fear the loss of, or—by projection—to fear harming in another. This absence allows the hysterical projections of a settled, critical discourse. Because the subject of violence has been deprived of a voice, "we" feel free, even compelled, to speak for him. But this presumption leads to an apparent impasse: on the one hand the deadly silence of the interrogated body; on the other, the inflationary sublimations of postmodern theory.

Referring to the systemic sources of violence, a Detroit prosecutor explained that

> This [violence] is not surprising for a number of obvious reasons: Drugs are almost everywhere, guns are available and school drop-outs. When you take kids who are uneducated, unskilled and uninterested and place them in a high-risk environment where easy money is to be made through criminal activity and the criminal justice system is without great accountability—well, you're going to have the problems we have now. (Swickard 5E)

The prosecutor's point is that there is a logic to this system, though not a narrative one; events are presided over and (albeit passively) regulated by local, state, and federal agencies. Consequently, the actual subject of violence knows very clearly what to do and how to act. That violence is a comprehensible element of his subjective economy, rather than an interruption of it, is an "obvious" fact, perhaps, though one not adequately grasped by many commentators. An interrogation seems clearly to have gone on, then, in Scarry's terms. Thus the chilled silence of people like Duane.

The process that Scarry identifies in a specific way with torture is, in fact, in less extreme terms, common to middle-class institutions generally. Of necessity, these institutions attack—"deconstruct" in her terms—the very subject that they ostensibly serve. And this process goes forward just as Scarry theorizes, "miming," or "objectifying in the external environment" the mechanism of interrogation. This aspect of interrogation becomes immediately obvious in the classic department store. In terms of the *culture* there represented, the store's purpose was ostensibly didactic and benign, as an early review of Marshall Field's suggests, with the store being compared to a "school" and a "museum." And undoubtedly the store—like a school or museum—did teach its subjects; it instructed them in correct choosing and *covered* the overt commercialism of this project by returning the symbolically negotiable accomplishment of "culture." In fact, however, Scarry's "interrogation" is a more accurate description of what actually occurred. Consider the logistics of the store interior. As I have suggested, classic shopping was a narrative process, one carefully managed by the store and its employees, who become stand-ins for the *individual* whom shoppers seek to become. The pedagogical end of this instructional project, however, is not some fixed individuality. On the contrary, the finished individual of the store is deprived of voice and history alike.

As if to flaunt its power, the classic store, like the interrogator, always made visible its deconstructive practice. Such stores were organized, or plotted, so as to lead up to the furniture department, which embodied the material good life the individual presumably aspired to and had been trained to inhabit. There, for the first time, space was no longer departmentalized; instead, the store apparently invited the contemplation of a whole life. But that was the same place where individuality and narrative alike dissolved, as mapping devices. This was the one site in the store, for example, where characterological stand-ins—mannequins—did not appear. Contrary to expectation, this was not where the now fully instructed individual came to exercise his own judgment, write his *own* story. Just the opposite: this was where the successfully interrogated subject finally embraced the interrogator, in the person of the "interior designer."

This process, as I suggested, is common to both store and mall: both institutionalize a subjectivity that they simultaneously attack. For the store, it was the narrative individual; for the mall, the sensate body. Just as the store was always interrogating—doing and undoing—time, the mall conducts an interrogation of space concurrent with the self-renewing operations of Tres Vite. The mall shows everything, all at once. It makes visible the consumer's domination of objects and of the old narrative of shopping. Specifically, it locates the body in a position of spatial superiority. But the spatial invitation of the mall is false, a disguised interrogation, just like the narrative invitation of the store. With this difference, however: the mall is not so much about learning as it is about historical memory.

The mall has only to mobilize the recollected situation of subjects in order to accomplish its errands because the symbolic economy of mall culture is precisely that of television coverage. The mall shows everyone visually just what is going on, in the same way that TV does. Nothing hidden here. But this apparent visual mastery is merely a cover for an interrogative deconstruction that goes forward, now uncriticized and unopposed, thanks to the accustomed dominance of sight over the other senses. As Luce Irigaray argues: "More than the other senses, the eye objectifies and masters. It sets at a distance, maintains the distance. In our culture, the predominance of the look over smell, taste, touch, hearing, has brought about an impoverishment of bodily relations. . . . The moment the look dominates, the body loses its materiality" (Owens 70). Just as with television, the eye dominates the rest of the sensate body, leading to the impression that "you are there," when only your sight has made the visit.

The point of such informational interrogations is to silence the witness of the other senses and so deconstruct the body, which is ostensibly being offered mastery over its own location in space. In this sense, the mall bears witness to its own success; it demonstrates the real impossibility of a "visit," to use Michel Serres's term—a term by which he means to engage the body as an ensemble of all its five senses. "To see without 'visiting,'" Thomas Kavanagh has said, with reference to Serres, "to see only with the eye, to indulge the proud sight of theory and its inevitable complicity with language, must be refused because it brings with it the murder of a reality which is always local, multiple, circumstantial, and *mélangé.* In its place, the imperium of sight and theory beholds only an homogeneous, isotropic, and panoramic space" (453). Significantly, Kavanagh and Serres note the complicity of theory—specifically the varieties of postmodern literary theory—with the silencing of the body. The critical body is always absent, covered by the *insight* of language, so that visits to the mall are no more genuine than those of the simulacra for whom the theoretician proposes to speak. Both are products of the same interrogation.

As to the working out of this interrogation, consider the mall shops. Just as with the individual in the store, the body is now dissolved at the site of its supposed authorization. Thanks to the false imperium of (in)sight, the body is silenced rather than invoked. Classic shopping has now been seen through, and along with it the temporal discipline associated with consumer objects, which the mall arrays randomly, "ironically," in the sense of TV. But what does this insight really count for? Rather than inviting a critique by the senses, it renders the body silent. For example, the mall ostensibly exists for the comfort and convenience of the individual body, yet nowhere is genuine comfort available. Just the reverse: under the cover of its putative insights, the mall appropriates the body and dulls the sensorium of subjects who might otherwise resist appropriation. "Mallaise," as one critic has referred to it (Kowinski 335–42), overtakes the subject producing a passivity like that induced by prolonged TV watching, so that the history of the body, as sensate ensemble, is humiliated into silence.

This accounts for the lurid, compensatory gestures of popular journalism and television, the "tabloid" fascination with the perils of the body: sexual terror, murder, mutilation, disfigurement, horrible accidents. The fascination is neither all gratuitous, however, nor even perhaps primarily so. On the contrary, there is evident here a terrible longing for an authentic visit: one that would reanimate the humiliated body by conjuring its presence viscerally, by literally turning it inside out and so provoking the witness of the other senses as to induce the overthrow of imperial insight. This explains the otherwise inexplicable, and possibly objectionable, proliferation of special-effects violence in films such as *Batman*, where it might otherwise seem gratuitous and irrelevant. But even in "action" pictures like *Terminator* and *Robocop*, where violence is now to be expected, certain prohibitions remain, so that the films never really get down to the work they appear to invite. These prohibitions are suspended, generically, in so-called "splatter movies," whose only point *is* violence. Various cycles, each with its own maniac, play to packed houses of adolescents at mall theaters, where the putative victims of horror come to discover, as entertainment, the rhetoric of their own real jeopardy.

Perhaps the most interesting of these films, and surely among the most successful, are *A Nightmare on Elm Street* (1984) and its various sequels. The "hero," who is also the natural historian of the mall, is Freddy Kreuger. Freddy not only lives at the mall, he behaves like it as well. He appropriates the visible body of his subjects, turning them into service sites for the performance of multiple special effects. But with this difference: the *Nightmare* films continue, and continue to be popular, because the individuals in them are able to defeat Freddy. This is what makes him different from the first-generation splatter maniacs, Jason of the *Friday the 13th* cycle and Michael Myers of *Halloween*, both of whom had lapsed into camp humor long before their exploits were completed. That fate seems not to have overtaken Freddy, whose methods are more sophisticated, visually as well as theoretically. The point of violence for him is to problematize the culturally central question of representation itself, in terms of both reference (is it real?) and politics (should we be seeing this?). In this way, violence is much more useful and powerful than graphic sex, which is the preoccupation of the first-generation splatter plots. With sex, we may be surprised at what is shown, but except for the question of body doubling (do you think this or that actor would do a nude scene?) representation itself goes uninterrogated. In the Freddy movies, however, seeing and believing are perpetually at odds. The eye is always getting the other senses into trouble, taking them where they shouldn't be and then when the crisis comes abandoning them to shift for themselves, which is right where Freddy wants them: where he's free to go all the way, as he could not do in the context of a "quality" picture.

Freddy comes at his victims in their dreams. Back when he was really alive, he murdered a lot of children on Elm Street; then when it came time to convict him, the courts did what they always do these days (or rather what they did in America before the Reagan/Bush judiciary arrived): they let him off through some legal loophole or other. So, it's up to angry parents to do the right thing. They soak Freddy and his hideout in gasoline and burn him to death. But Freddy isn't to be gotten over, any more than the sleeping horrors of liberalism. Now he comes back to Elm Street to haunt the dreams of the teenage sons and daughters of the vigilante parents, and it's there—in dreams—that Freddy makes his mischief. Now terribly disfigured by his burns and sporting a prosthetic hand comprised of four razor-like blades, he forces the kids to dream their own ultra-violent deaths, from which they actually die. That's the plot more or less.

But plot is not really the point. Over and over again the point is the history of visits, in Serres's terms. As I've suggested, Freddy's project is perpetually to embarrass the eyes and humiliate their imperial insights. The films do this thematically, by refusing to resolve the question of which scenes are real and which are dreams in much the same way that *Batman* makes intentional the figure/ground ambiguity on which Gotham is founded. But rather than stopping here, Freddy uses this as a starting place for his house calls. The visual interrogation of the body, which is common to television and shopping mall, is itself played backward now, so as to restore the competence of a body whose sensory ensemble has been canceled. For this purpose, the films have to be highly inventive in their application of special effects. Freddy is endlessly imaginative when it comes to theorizing and eviscerating his victims, which leads to a renewal of the body in spectators, whose five senses are constantly being appealed to, confronted, assaulted, *grossed out*, in that telling phrase. And in each case, the failure of the eyes to manage, to interrogate, the body leads to this renewal of the other senses. If the eyes were as smart as they think they are, in other words, or as smart as we have been institutionally led to believe, none of this would happen. That the eyes are not in control of the body is the message repeated by the Freddy films and their clones. In that way, they are discovering a *new* history of the senses—one beyond the reach of theoretical insight.

For that reason, perhaps, the same kids who become victims in these films also make up their audience, and for the same reason that patrons pay to be turned inside out at Tres Vite: because in the experience of interrogation there resides—potentially—a powerful moment of self-recognition, an opening for the *refusal* of "insight." And in both instances, these commercially packaged experiences are merely bland recuperations of the subject under interrogation by actual violence, a violence that, for many, has become continuous with urban culture. The inevitable failure of language at this precise moment of insight leads to a nostalgia for a speech that does not yet exist, but which must be invented, under interrogation, if the history that comes after history is ever to find voice. Thus the obsessive return of our society to stories of horror and violation because we have lost the old distinctions of outside and inside that once made the narratively constituted body (whether individual or the body politic) a fit subject for conservation. It is impossible to conserve what is not understood, so that new means of discovery will be necessary if the individual body is once again to become the subject of desirable, and communicable, visits.

## V: Two Bums

This is only to say that people who left the city are now playing a kind of elective catch-up with the dearly priced intelligence of those who couldn't find a way out. I have this lesson explained to me one afternoon while I am riding home from work on the bus. I take a seat in front of two bums who appear to be wearing every piece of clothing they own because the weather is very cold, and they must spend the day getting periodically turned out into it. As I settle into my spot, I can overhear one of them explaining something to his companion, who seems to be dozing; it's a lesson about art, which probably reflects where the two men have spent the afternoon—at the Detroit Institute of Arts, the stop just before mine. "Now at your DIA," the first man says, "you've got your five kinds of pictures. Your masterpiece, your very good, your good, your OK, and your poor." The man being spoken to is snoring. "Got that?" his friend asks, reviewing the lesson, "Your masterpiece, your very good, your good, your OK, and your poor." "Nargle gargle," the man answers. "Isn't that right?" the bum says, tapping me on the shoulder. He is patient when I adopt the mannerly pose of not having heard his already twice repeated recitation. He holds his hand up and ticks off the lesson on gloved fingers, "Your masterpiece, your very good, your good, your OK, and your poor? The five kinds of pictures?"

I nod my head in affirmation, but this endorsement is not so enthusiastic as he'd hoped for, so the bum abandons his friend, whose head is now lolling, open-mouthed, against the seat back. The man has found a more interesting, live prospect in me. I realize at once the mistake I've made; it's a greenhorn's error to respond to street people when they talk, let alone to get pinned by one in a seat, as the man has now pinned me in mine, leaving his friend to shift for himself behind us. "So, who's your best painter?" he wants to know, fixing me with a more focused, critical attention. It's impossible to pretend that I am not having a conversation with this man, who in the stuffy heat of the bus has begun to put off an odor like over-ripe Camembert. "Who?" he demands. He is wearing a black eye patch that he now flips up to reveal—not some terrible wound, thank God, but just another bloodshot eye that he apparently needs the help of to execute an effective scrutiny.

"Rembrandt," I tell him, hoping I've picked a name he'll recognize and so leave me alone. "Too dark," he snorts, condescendingly, and because I don't turn away quickly enough, he interprets eye contact as an invitation to continue. "The lacquer gets old, turns the pictures dark, makes them hard to clean. And besides," he continues, "there aren't any good ones at the museum. Their Rembrandts are little, no account." He wants me to try again, but he's willing to help out because I obviously know very little about art, and the local museum. "Who's your best *live* painter," he coaches me: "DIA has lots of good live ones." "Frank Stella," I tell the man, wondering if he will remember the wall-sized piece in the twentieth-century collection, for which the DIA is in fact duly famous. "Third-rate crap," the bum sniffs. His friend, who has waked up, is leaning over the seat back between us. "What you do?" he asks me with obviously slurred speech. I tell him I work at the university. "Building and grounds?" the first bum inquires. "Grounds," he repeats, a little irritated, when I say I don't understand, "You a janitor?" It's then that I notice we're both wearing the same army surplus overcoat, except his seems newer and less frayed than mine. I find myself wanting to explain this isn't my real overcoat; it's just an old one, from graduate school, that I still wear sometimes in weather like this. Instead, I tell him I'm a teacher. "Wha you deach?" the sidekick wants to know. I say I'm an English professor, as I reach up to pull the cord and signal the driver that we're approaching my stop. I get up to leave, and as I exit through the back door, my interlocutor, who has made way for me and is now standing too, executes an elaborate, sweeping bow, which he concludes with a flourish by flipping his eye patch histrionically shut.

Later, I recount this improbable conversation to friends, who are used to hearing my stories about the city. I get the laugh I was looking for. One friend in particular, an art historian who works at the DIA, likes the anecdote so much he has me repeat it at a dinner party at his house. The guests—a couple of museum people, a photographer, a toy designer, a hospital administrator, a librarian—are appreciative. The real pay-off comes when one woman asks, a little incredulous, if I really ride the city buses. "Every day," I tell her, preening in what I imagine to be her admiration for my urban pluck. What I don't tell her is that my daily ride is only a mile long, and that after ten years the worst I can say about the buses is that I've frequently had to wait, or been crowded in, and that I often get talked to by people I don't know, some of whom are drunk, or drugged (both therapeutically and recreationally), some of whom just want another person to listen. The line I ride is a "good" one, though, right down Woodward; with buses scheduled every seven minutes, even in the worst weather the wait is usually not more than twice that. Everybody who lives here is not so lucky.

Like the coat that is not my real coat, these commuter visits of mine are not real visits either—visits in Serres's sense. If Tom Kavanagh had heard my little story, in other words, he might have wanted to chide me along with the literary theoreticians: "to see only with the eye, to indulge the proud sight of theory and its inevitable complicity with language, must be refused because it brings with it the murder of a reality which is always local, multiple, circumstantial, and *mélangé*" (453). If the weather is too bad, or the bus is late, or if I just don't feel like dealing with company that is *mélangé*, I raise my arm and hail a taxi, and because of how I look (even when I'm wearing my old coat), one stops right away, and none of the drivers ever asks to see my money "up front." The two bums and I ride the same bus, then, but not in the same body; I am informed by other options, necessities, cares, so that our coming into contact ends—inevitably, it seems—in a kind of mutual humiliation, which is the meaning of the man's histrionic final bow. It's no less what I do to him, of course, with the self-aggrandizing little story, which turns to humorous account the knowledge he's paid for so dearly in the body.

The problem of the city, then, at least in some ways, is much as it has always been; it's the same problem that confronted Howells a hundred years ago: the problem of sustaining a representation at the precise vanishing point of history. What is the city to stand for, in other words, if it is always covering its own past and converting memory to some new capital opportunity? The city of information, to which I belong—the vertical, second city of selective, renewable entries—is parasitic on the old, first city of history, so that when it goes, I wonder how I will locate my own life whose profoundest history is written in the humiliation of that remaindered, non-renewable other.

On the near east side of Detroit, an artist, Tyree Guyton, has arrived—physically—at something like this same conclusion, and he has been made to pay for the revelation vouchsafed in his found-art sculptures. Guyton was born in 1955 and grew up in a house on Heidelberg Street, which by the 1980s had gone the way of many streets in Detroit. What had once been an ethnic, working-class neighborhood became a mostly African-American neighborhood on which depopulation, poverty, and finally crack took its toll. The street was in poor condition, with abandoned houses being used by addicts, dealers, and prostitutes; it was dangerous to walk here, day or night. Then, according to a story in *Newsweek* magazine,

> Guyton, 34, enlisted his wife, Karen, and his grandfather, Sam Mackey, and began to transform a dilapidated area on Detroit's east side into a kind of living art gallery. . . . A bathtub in a vacant lot becomes a cornucopia of tires, fenders and road signs, and old bicycles dangle from tree limbs to compose a half-natural, half-artificial sculpture. But the *pièces de résistance* are two abandoned houses festooned with everything from dolls to phone booths. (64)

The account is an accurate representation, as far as it goes. But description can only go so far in conveying the impact of Guyton's project. His houses literally vomit forth the physical elements of domestic history; furniture, dolls, television sets, signs, toilets, enema bottles, beds, tires, baby buggies come cascading out doors and windows and through holes in the roof, flowing down the outside walls and collecting in great heaps on the lawn, so that the whole looks like some sort of man-made lava flow. The magma of discarded lives: these visible tokens of a humiliated history.

In that sense, Guyton has constructed a shrewd parody of the inside/out logic of renewal. He has done for the poor what conversion does for the middle class. Like the little boutiques and restaurants that occupy the formerly domestic areas of historic interiors, Guyton's "Project" similarly converts private space to public spectacle. But the results in his case are not so much reassuring as they are disturbing. It is impossible to look at the Heidelberg Project and not imagine that something terrible has happened to cause this explosion of physical deformity. And of course something has. Perhaps the most visible witness to this fact is the profusion of dolls, which are both incorporated in the design of the houses, and also nailed up in trees, or used as parts of free-standing sculptures. But invariably, the dolls are mangled and mutilated, figural representatives of the once desirable, and now humiliated objects that surround them: their arms are missing, or their heads; they are hung upside down as if victims of some dreadful sacrifice. To visit Tyree's neighborhood is to visit the body specifically as dismembered witness to the humiliations of historical interrogation.

The notoriety of his project was such that he accomplished, virtually singlehanded, a remarkable kind of urban renewal. As the catalog for an exhibition of his work at the Detroit Institute of Arts noted in 1990, the level of traffic generated by news about the Project has helped turn the formerly dangerous neighborhood around:

> Guyton's art seems to invoke safety, connectedness, meaning, and a sense of continuity between past and present. Through his art, Guyton is transforming a hard-core inner-city neighborhood where peo-

> ple were afraid to walk, even in the daytime, to one in which neighbors take pride and where visitors are many and welcome. The blocks around Heidelberg and Mt. Elliott have changed from a "war zone" to a "sanctuary of wonder," from an area devoid of people to one where people come gladly with fascination and energy. (Jackson 7)

Here the discourse of art-historical connoisseurship translates Guyton to "safety, connectedness, meaning, and a sense of continuity between past and present." It is questionable whether anybody would have bothered looking at his houses in the first place if that was what they're really about. But the museum is a representational institution, whose mission is to convert to aesthetic solutions the otherwise problematic witness of history, so that the visits Tyree invites on Heidelberg Street, that helped turn his neighborhood around, are not the same ones memorialized at the DIA.

The city of Detroit was not so obtuse in its appreciation of Guyton's work. In 1989 a municipal crew demolished, without notice, one of Guyton's first projects "Babydoll House," at a time when there were over 15,000 abandoned structures throughout the city. That demolition was followed, two years later, in November 1991, by a demolition of the remaining houses in the Heidelberg Project. Crews arrived early one Saturday morning, as part of their "regularly scheduled work," and tore the houses down before anything could be done to prevent them, which makes rather dubious the art historian's claim that Guyton's work is about "safety, connectedness, meaning." If that were the case, then there would have been little point in demolishing his houses. Detroit poet John Sinclair wrote a piece, prior to the demolition, in which he celebrates Guyton and his fondness for Thelonious Monk and John Coltrane and makes clear the reason why the houses had to go:

> the music comes up in the background
> out of the little speaker
> on the radio by the porch, it's thelonious
>
> with charlie rouse, "monk's dream"
> & the peoples indoors sleeping

turn over in they beds,

a smile on they faces,
they know in their dreams
it's just tyree & grandpop out there

on heidelberg street
in the middle of the night
turning their neighborhood inside out.

By "turning their neighborhood inside out," Guyton and his wife and grandfather mock the failure of the historical city to conserve either objects or people; they humiliate the presumptive authority of representative culture. This is why their material insights have themselves been submitted to violent erasure: because in the city of renewals, only the converted will be allowed a history.

# Conclusion

## Taking Leave

After all that has been said and done, what could there possibly be left to say about Detroit? As it turns out, quite a lot. This city that has—by common agreement—ceased to exist refuses apparently to go away. Detroit stands for an America that is over: the America of gas guzzlers and factories and downtown and department stores and above all the America where people believed that the good of the country and the good of General Motors were inextricably linked. That America, and the city that stood for it, are exhausted, so that Motown now seems apropos of nothing so much as failure, with everybody wanting to have the last word, not one of which appears sufficient to the task of really being the last. Not too long ago, the editors of the *Nation*, for example, thought it necessary to remind their readers that Detroit was still "Detroit":

> Detroit confronts the visitor and resident alike with ubiquitous decay. The downtown contains the most awesome concentration of emerging ruins in the nation: prematurely aging skyscrapers stripped by their owners and abandoned to nature. Seen from the north, beyond the wide gap of the Fisher Freeway, a cluster of mostly empty Art Deco office buildings rises hundreds of feet above cleared lots. In its shadow, low buildings draw the homeless, alcoholics, drug addicts and others to institutions set up to help them. Large numbers of people congregate in only a few places: near the Detroit River, on a narrow strip about two blocks wide; and in Greektown, an enclave of ethnic restaurants and shops. (Vergara 660–61)

This entirely unremarkable version of Detroit (excerpted from yet another upcoming book) goes on to recount all the, by now, expectable oppositions: *then* versus *now*, industrial power versus postindustrial failure, white versus black, suburb versus city. It elides what doesn't fit—the redevelopment of downtown and the river front, with two new skyscrapers and a notable influx of Japanese capital—and gets on with the odd business of discovery.

The effect Detroit has on people—particularly writers—is like what seems to have been the effect Pompeii had on the Victorians. "City of the dead, city of the dead," Thackeray couldn't stop telling anybody who would listen, as if he were expecting something different. Each person to see this town feels he's somehow discovered it and has a consequent obligation to rush home and report. As to that, there's no denying the power of the place, particularly at first sight. It is impossible to convey the eerie effect of so much real property—houses, department stores, office towers, theaters, shops, schools, apartment buildings, hospitals, hotels, fire houses, mansions, streets, fountains, factories, whole neighborhoods—having simply been left behind, as if the inhabitants were carried off by some terrible natural disaster. Detroit is a worst-case illustration that seemingly demands an explanatory caption, with everybody getting a chance to ward off his own special demons by abandoning them to speculation here.

There's that, and there's also the concomitant invitation to brag, which is summed up nicely by a tee-shirt that local vendors sell.

"I'm so bad," the shirt's inscription reads, "I party in Detroit." "For two weeks," Vergara wrote in the *Nation*,

> I lived in the city's desolate northwest [*sic*] section, immediately west of Grand Circus Park. . . . The sinister Book Tower, the tallest building in the area, looks like something out of a science-fiction novel. With almost no tenants, its 350-foot height serves mainly to support communications equipment. A brilliant white dish antenna on its classical temple top seems like a gigantic, wide-open eye surveying the city. A forest of rusting metal poles rises from the roof. On the streets, wanderers and madmen sit on the sidewalks or push shopping carts. (662)

For six years, I lived at the Grand Circus Park, which is still one of the prettiest parts of the city, and the one that comes closest to realizing Judge Augustus Woodward's plan for Detroit, which he copied in 1807 from L'Enfant's layout of Washington, D.C. The Book Building—an ornate thirteen-story block with adjacent thirty-six story tower—is really quite wonderful, in a literal sense: it makes you wonder what could have been on the minds of its architect, Louis Kamper, and the Book brothers—Herbert, Frank, and J. Burgess, Jr.—when they devised the design, with columns and urns and the twelve nude carytids who support the cornice. I used to sit in my apartment across the street and stare with binoculars at the marvelous detailing, which at ground level nobody of course can possibly see. As for Vergara's "wanderers and madmen," they are mostly old, long-term inmates of institutions, who get dumped on the streets in spring, like some tragic human version of Reaganomic crocuses. Last week, when I was at Grand Circus Park to visit my dentist, they were—happily—not in evidence as the two of us walked across the Park to get lunch at the Detroit Athletic Club. Or maybe I wasn't paying attention to the wanderers and madmen specifically. Each person has his own special fears, and his own special pride at having faced them down, so my Detroit isn't going to be precisely like anybody else's.

Which is not to say that Vergara is wrong about the city, or that Ze'ev Chafets was wrong in *Devil's Night*, or that any of the other people who have felt—or will feel—compelled to "discover" Detroit are going to be wrong in what they find. Their efforts seem honest, if fraught with a fascinating superfluity: Why tell the same sad story again? When it comes to that, the citizens of this place are no better than anybody else. There is *Detroit Images* (1989), for example, subtitled "Photographs of the Renaissance City," which must surely be the most depressing and peculiar coffee-table book ever produced about a city. In it, nineteen photographers have assembled a collection of unrelievedly gloomy and desolate "images": of riots, abandoned houses, collapsed buildings, crumbling theaters, welfare hotels and their impoverished residents, demolitions, industrial wrecks, stripped autos. As the introduction proudly proclaims, "All but one of the photographers represented in *Detroit Images* have lived in Detroit or its immediate environs for much of their lives, and many of them were raised in the city" (28). In the "Afterword," the poet Philip Levine, also a native Detroiter, pointed out the obvious. "This is in fact a book of ruins," he wrote:

> A war was fought here. American capitalism, armed with greed, racism, and the design for the world's gaudiest fish-tailed Cadillac took on the land, the air, and the people, and we all lost. . . . I suppose we should be thankful we have no aerial photographs, for they might very well remind us of Dresden after the firebombing. . . . (257)

So why produce this "gallery of the defeated," as he has called it? Why overstate—however artfully—what is so painfully obvious?

It's because the longer you look at this place, the greater the loss there is to account for; and it's impossible not to take the loss personally, particularly if you are white and middle class and not bound to remain here, except in memory. And it's there, in memory, that Detroit exists, for the majority of its citizens, who have chosen long since to live somewhere else. But taking leave of the place is not so easy as just changing an address, which is the point Levine makes, quite eloquently, in closing his expatriate's reflections:

> I see the lights of a city that gave me a life I loved, a place I called mine and came back to year after year until I could no longer find it. In this collection of photographs I possess a portion of all that survived, wounded, complex, turbulent, this great piece of America that refuses to go away. As long as the boy and young man are alive in me, I'll carry it with me as it was, a city of wonder, the place of first loss, my home. (260)

"This great piece of America that refuses to go away": that's the problem with Detroit. People who become witnesses to the city can't *not* remember the enormity of what has been lost here. They find themselves turning back upon it with an almost vengeful wish to get even, to banish the pain of memory, and what has become of remembered things, which perhaps accounts for the bleak erasure of *Detroit Images*.

It surely accounts for Lawrence Joseph's brilliant poetic memoir, *Shouting At No One*. Again and again the poet is humiliated by the memory of a past that exists nowhere but there, in memory, and that impoverishes his life by its refusal to disappear; it's Levine's same memory of the city he "called mine and came back to year after year until I could no longer find it." Joseph's shout, in "It's Not Me Shouting at No One," is a protest against the helplessness of such recollection:

> Always four smokestacks
> burning bones, somewhere
> tears that won't stop,
> everywhere blood becomes
> flesh that wants to say something.
> It's not me shouting at no one
> in Cadillac Square: it's God
> roaring inside me, afraid
> to be alone. (55)

I know of no other place that inspires such a fierce and dreadful nostalgia. Of course, there is no other place so completely vanished as this one, where only the tourists are let off the hook, and not even all of them are spared, as Vergara's example makes clear.

I have lived here long enough myself now, after ten years, to have begun feeling something like a native's dread of recollection. I find myself getting lost, sometimes, in memories of places, and lives, that neglect and abandonment have laid waste and destroyed. It would not be possible, for example, to reproduce many of the visits that I have written about here because the shops and theaters and stores—and the people—no longer exist, or if they do, it's only as ruins of what was there before, which puts me in company with the blue-haired lady I ran into that spring afternoon when she'd gotten lost in her own hometown. This is not to say that everything here is falling apart, because it is not; or that there isn't redevelopment going on, because there is, with Tres Vite and the Elwood being prime examples. But the fact remains that nowhere else in this country has so much history, both human and material, been reduced to a dreadful and frightening inconsequence.

And that is what makes the city so vulnerable to the last forms of looting, which have all to do with the opportune theft of memory. Lest I'd forgotten this simple, if humbling, truth, a messenger was sent to admonish me not long ago. I'd just boarded the Dexter bus, inbound; as we left the stop at Henry Ford Hospital, heading east on Grand Boulevard toward the Fisher Building and GM World Headquarters, I was accosted by one of Vergara's "madmen," this one an apparent schizophrenic who had skipped, or else run out of his medication. The man was large, in his sixties probably, and obviously poor, although his clothes were neat and looked as if they might have been given to him at a half-way house, of which there are many in this neighborhood. I started to take the empty seat next to his, but he made it clear that was a wrong idea, so I moved further down the aisle. He fixed me with his wild stare, growing obviously more upset, until all at once he jumped to his feet and reached for his weapon, which was a length of worn fan belt clasped between two floppy pieces of cardboard. He drew the fan belt from its makeshift scabbard, and held it aloft, like a wilted broadsword.

I'd just been musing over the fact that this was among the last bus rides I would take in Detroit because I'd recently bought a car, which I was now waiting to pick up from the dealer. I wouldn't be leaving the city exactly, at least not yet, although I'd spent a good deal of time in the winter talking to real estate agents and looking at suburban houses. But I would be visiting it in a different way—alone, in my car, on the kind of site-specific trips that people who don't ride buses come to think of as natural. "I know who you are," the madman shouted, preparing to defend himself. The woman sitting across the aisle turned to her friend. "Don't you just hate the spring," she said, talking loudly enough so that I could hear too, "Don't you just hate it when they turn all them people out of doors." "I know who you are," the man screamed and started my way: "Don't come around here checking on me." We'd just reached the next stop, and people had begun to board; the bus driver got up and took hold of my inquisitor. "You want help?" he demanded, his face only inches away from the man's. It was obvious from the man's wild stare that the question was meaningless to him; he bolted through the open door of the bus and ran across a freeway ramp where he was nearly struck by on-coming traffic. He made it to the other side, though, and jumped through the back door of a departing bus, just as it took off.

I can't help thinking about the man, and about the city that I've lived in and looked at and written about now that I'm taking my leave of both, at least metaphorically, with the writing about them being almost done. The man had a right to defend himself, for fear of how he might be used. But life had deprived him of the resources that a real defense would require. History has been only slightly more generous to Detroit. Which is to say, it's easy to make a "madman" of that sad, humiliated life, just as it's easy to find "true tales" to tell about this city. And it's understandable that people would want to do so: to keep their guilts and fears and anxieties at bay. I think about the madman, then, and I know he wasn't shouting at no one. He was talking to me.

# Bibliography

Aldrich, Nelson W., Jr. *Old Money: The Mythology of America's Upper Class.* New York: Knopf, 1988.

Allis, Sam. "Contrary to Previous Reports, Cities Are Not Dead." *Time*, 7 Aug. 1989, 9–10.

Altman, Rick. "Television/Sound." *Studies in Entertainment: Critical Approaches to Mass Culture*, ed. Tania Modleski. Bloomington: Indiana University Press, 1986. 39–54.

Auster, Paul. *City of Glass.* New York: Penguin, 1987.

Baker, Nicholson. *The Mezzanine.* New York: Weidenfeld & Nicholson, 1988.

Banks, Russell. *Continental Drift.* New York: Ballantine Books, 1985.

Barron, John. "New Frontiers: Where Do You Fit In?" *Detroit Monthly*, March 1990, 52–59.

Barthes, Roland. *Image Music Text.* Trans. Stephen Heath. New York: Hill and Wang, 1977.

———. "The Realistic Effect." *Film Reader* 3 (1978): 134+.

Baudrillard, Jean. "The Ecstasy of Communication." Trans. John Johnston. *The Anti-Aesthetic: Essays on Postmodern Culture.* Ed. Hal Foster. Port Townsend, Wash.: Bay Press, 1983. 126–34.

Baxter, Charles. "The Passionate Shopping Mall." *Imaginary Paintings.* Latham, N.Y.: Paris Review Editions, 1989. 7–8.

Bennett, Edward H. "The City Plan of Detroit." *Proceedings of the Seventh National Conference on City Planning, Detroit June 7–9, 1915.* Boston: University Press, 1915. 21–32.

Bhabha, Homi K. "The Commitment to Theory." *New Formations* 5 (Summer 1988): 10–11.

Birmingham, Nan Tillson. *Store.* New York: G. P. Putnam's Sons, 1978.

Bogue, Ronald. "Pasta, Barthes and Baudrillard." *Bucknell Review* 27.1 (1982): 125–39.

Braudy, Leo. "In the Arts, Tomorrow Begins With Yesterday." *New York Times*, natl. ed., 1 July 1990, 2.1+.

Bukowczyk, John J., and Douglas Aikenhead, with Peter Slavcheff, eds. *Detroit Images: Photographs of the Renaissance City.* Detroit: Wayne State University Press, 1989.

Calvino, Italo. *Invisible Cities.* Trans. William Weaver. New York: Harcourt Brace Jovanovich, 1974.

Chafets, Ze'ev. *Devil's Night and Other True Tales of Detroit.* New York: Random House, 1990.

———. "The Tragedy of Detroit." *New York Times Magazine*, 29 July 1990, 20–26, 38, 42, 50–51.

Chesley, Roger. "Shoot-out Claims Life of High School Freshman." *Detroit Free Press*, 4 July 1992, A3.

Clifford, James. *The Predicament of Culture: Twentieth-Century Ethnography, Literature, and Art.* Cambridge: Harvard University Press, 1988.

Debord, Guy. *Society of the Spectacle.* Detroit: Black & Red, 1983. (There are no page numbers; instead, entries are numbered separately.)

de Certeau, Michel. *The Practice of Everyday Life.* Trans. Steven Rendall. Berkeley: University of California Press, 1988.

de Man, Paul. *Blindness and Insight: Eight Essays in the Rhetoric of Contemporary Criticism.* 2d. ed. Minneapolis: University of Minnesota Press, 1983.

"Derailed by Success." *Time*, 25 June 1990, 25.

Derrida, Jacques. *Of Grammatology.* Trans. Gayatri Chakravorty Spivak. Baltimore: Johns Hopkins University Press, 1976.

"Detroit's Agony," on "Prime Time Live." ABC. 8 Nov. 1990.

"Detroit's Torn Lifeline." *Newsweek*, 3 Sept. 1984, 59.

Doctorow, E. L. *Ragtime.* New York: Random House, 1975.

Dreiser, Theodore. *Sister Carrie.* New York: New American Library, 1961.

Ehrenreich, Barbara. *Fear of Falling: The Inner Life of the Middle Class.* New York: Pantheon, 1989.

Ferry, W. Hawkins. *The Buildings of Detroit.* Rev. ed. Detroit: Wayne State University Press, 1980.

Fitzgerald, F. Scott. *The Great Gatsby.* New York: Charles Scribner's Sons, 1925.

Garreau, Joel. *Edge City: Life on the New Frontier.* New York: Doubleday, 1991.

Glynn, Thomas. *Building.* New York: Knopf, 1986.

Goldberger, Paul. "Why Design Can't Transform Cities." *New York Times,* natl. ed., 25 June 1989, 2.1+.

Gómez-Peña, Guillermo. "Border Culture: A Process of Negotiation Toward Utopia." Trans. by Emily Hicks and Gustavo Segade in *The Broken Line/La Linea Quebrada* 1 (May 1986): unpaginated.

Gottdiener, Mark. *The Social Production of Urban Space.* Austin: University of Texas Press, 1985.

Herr, Michael. *Dispatches.* New York: Avon, 1980.

Herron, Jerry. "Chicago, Opening Day." *Raritan* 8.3 (1989): 55–71.

Hopkins, Carol. "Bruce in Your Face." *Detroit Monthly,* July 1990, 14.

Howells, William Dean. *A Hazard of New Fortunes.* Bloomington: Indiana University Press, 1976.

———. *A Modern Instance.* Bloomington: Indiana University Press, 1977.

Hunt, Don, and Mary Hunt. *Hunts' Guide to Southeast Michigan.* Waterloo, Mich.: Midwestern Guides, 1990.

Ingersoll, Brenda. "Horatio Algers Without Diplomas." *Detroit News,* 8 May 1989, B 1+.

Jackson, Kenneth T. *Crabgrass Frontier: The Suburbanization of the United States.* New York: Oxford University Press, 1985.

Jackson, Marion E. "Tyree Guyton: Listenin' to his Art." *Tyree Guyton.* Catalog of an exhibition at the Detroit Institute of Arts, 30 June–19 August 1990. Detroit: Founders Society Detroit Institute of Arts, 1990.

Jameson, Fredric. "Nostalgia for the Present." *South Atlantic Quarterly* 88.2 (1989): 517–37.

———. "Postmodernism, or The Cultural Logic of Late Capitalism." *New Left Review* 146 (1984): 53–92.

———. *Postmodernism, or, the Cultural Logic of Late Capitalism.* Durham, N.C.: Duke University Press, 1991.

Joseph, Lawrence. *Shouting At No One.* Pittsburgh: University of Pittsburgh Press,1983.

Katz, Diane. "Devastating Drug Toll Growing Daily." *Detroit News,* 24 Oct. 1988, A1, 4.

Kavanagh, Thomas M. "Uneasy Theories: The Ethics of Narration in Contemporary French Criticism." *Criticism* 28 (1986): 445–58.

Kowinski, William Severini. *The Malling of America: An Inside Look at the Great Consumer Paradise.* New York: William Morrow, 1985.

Lacayo, Richard. "This Land Is Your Land. . . . "*Time*, 18 May 1992, 28–33.

Lemann, Nicholas. "Naperville: Stressed Out in Suburbia." *Atlantic*, Nov. 1989, 34–48.

Lewis, Sinclair. *Babbitt.* New York: Signet, 1961.

"The lighter was Sandoz. . . . "*Playboy*, May 1990, 5.

Lyotard, Jean François. *The Postmodern Condition: A Report on Knowledge.* Trans. Geoff Bennington and Brian Massumi. Minneapolis: University of Minnesota Press, 1984.

McInerney, Jay. *Bright Lights, Big City.* New York: Vintage, 1984.

Markiewicz, David A. "Opa!" *Detroit News,*11 May 1992, F3+.

———. "Ratings Fail to Bowl Over TV Ad Buyers." *Detroit News* 30 Jan. 1990, A1+

May, Larry. *Screening Out the Past: The Birth of Mass Culture and the Motion Picture Industry.* Chicago: University of Chicago Press, 1983.

Melder, R. Eugene. "The Tin Lizzie's Golden Anniversary." *American Quarterly* 12 (Winter 1961): 469–71.

Miller, Mark Crispin. *Boxed In: The Culture of TV.* Evanston, Ill.: Northwestern University Press, 1988.

Morganthau, Tom, John McCormick, and Marc Levinson. "Are Cities Obsolete?" *Newsweek*, 9 Sept. 1991, 42–44.

Mumford, Lewis. *The City in History.* New York: Harcourt, Brace & World, 1961.

Naisbitt, John. *Megatrends: Ten New Directions Transforming Our Lives.* New York: Warner Books, 1984.

———, and Patricia Aburdene. *Re-inventing the Corporation: Transforming Your Job and Your Company for the New Information Society.* New York: Warner Books, 1985.

———, and Patricia Aburdene. *Megatrends 2000: Ten New Directions for the 1990's.* New York: William Morrow, 1990.

Newman, Charles. *The Post-Modern Aura: The Act of Fiction in an Age of Inflation.* Evanston, Ill.: Northwestern University Press, 1984.

Owens, Craig. "The Discourse of Others: Feminists and Postmodernism." *The Anti-Aesthetic: Essays on Postmodern Culture.* Ed. Hal Foster. Port Townsend, Wash.: Bay Press, 1986. 57–82.

"Own the Ultimate Coca-Cola Collectible." *The Sharper Image*, July 1990, 21.

Plagens, Peter, with Frank Washington. "Come On-a My House." *Newsweek*, 6 Aug. 1990, 64.

Pynchon, Thomas. *The Crying of Lot 49*. New York: Bantam, 1982.

Quaife, Milo M. *This is Detroit: 1701–1951, Two Hundred and Fifty Years in Pictures*. Detroit: Wayne University Press, 1951.

Quayle, Dan. "Excerpts From Vice President's Speech on Cities and Poverty." *New York Times*, natl. ed., 30 May 1992, A11.

*Report of the National Advisory Commission on Civil Disorders*. New York: Bantam Books, 1968.

"Restaurants." *Detroit Monthly*, Feb. 1992, 67–77.

Risen, James. "Pheasants Reclaiming Parts of Detroit Man Is Abandoning," *Ann Arbor News*, 14 Nov. 1988, A 14.

Roth, Philip. *Goodbye, Columbus*. New York: Bantam, 1970.

Rybczynski, Witold. Home: *A Short History of an Idea*. New York: Viking, 1986.

Samuelson, Robert J. "How Our American Dream Unraveled." *Newsweek*, 2 March 1992, 32–39.

Scarry, Elaine. *The Body in Pain: The Making and Unmaking of the World*. New York: Oxford University Press, 1985.

Schramm, Jack E., and William H. Henning. *Detroit's Street Railways*, 2 vols. Chicago: Central Electric Railfans' Association, 1978.

Sennett, Richard. *The Conscience of the Eye: The Design and Social Life of Cities*. New York: W. W. Norton, 1990.

———. Contributions in "Whatever Became of the Public Square?" *Harper's*, July 1990, 49–60.

———. "Plate Glass." *Raritan* 6.4 (1987): 1–15.

Serres, Michel. *Les Cinq Sens*. Paris: Grasset, 1985.

Sharpe, William, and Leonard Wallock. "From 'Great Town' to 'Nonplace Urban Realm': Reading the Modern City." *Visions of the Modern City: Essays in History, Art, and Literature*, ed. William Sharpe and Leonard Wallock. Baltimore: Johns Hopkins University Press, 1987. 1–50.

Silverman, Debora. *Selling Culture: Bloomingdale's, Diana Vreeland, and the New Aristocracy of Taste in Reagan's America*. New York: Pantheon, 1986.

Sinclair, John. "#107 Monk's Dream." Quoted in *Tyree Guyton*. Catalog of an exhibition at the Detroit Institute of Arts, 30 June–19 August 1990. Detroit: Founders Society Detroit Institute of Arts, 1990.

*The Social Secretary of Detroit.* Detroit: Social Secretary, 1924.
"Soundoff." *Detroit Free Press,* 24 June 1985, A13.
Stone, Michael. "What Really Happened in Central Park." *New York,* 14 Aug. 1989, 30–43.
Swickard, Joe. "Treating Shootings as a Disease: Health Experts Join Fight Against Youth Violence." *Detroit Free Press,* 18 Dec. 1988, E5.
Tafuri, Manfredo. *Architecture and Utopia: Design and Capitalist Development.* Trans. Barbara Luigia La Penta. Cambridge: MIT Press, 1976.
Toner, Robin. "Los Angeles Riots Are a Warning, Americans Fear." *New York Times,* natl. ed., 11 May 1992, 1.1+.
"Toronto and Detroit: Canadians Do It Better." *Economist* 315.7655 (19 May 1990): 17–20.
Towers, Robert. "The Flap Over Tom Wolfe: How Real Is the Retreat From Realism?" *New York Times Book Review* 28 Jan. 1990: 15–16.
Venturi, Robert, Denise Scott Brown, Steven Izenour. *Learning from Las Vegas: The Forgotten Symbolism of Architectural Form.* Rev. ed. Cambridge: MIT Press, 1988.
Vergara, Camilo José. "Postindustrial City: Detroit Waits for the Millennium." *The Nation,* 18 May 1992, 660–64.
Watt, Ian. *The Rise of the Novel.* Berkeley: University of California Press, 1971.
Watten, Barrett. "Direct Address." *Conduit.* San Francisco: GAZ, 1988. 57–76.
*Webster's New Collegiate Dictionary.* Springfield, Mass.: G. & C. Merriam, 1974.
Wolfe, Tom. *The Bonfire of the Vanities.* New York: Farrar, Straus, Giroux, 1987.
———. "(Intermission) Pause, Now, and Consider Some Tentative Conclusions About the Meaning of This Mass Perversion Called Porno-Violence: What It Is and Where It Comes From and Who Put the Hair on the Walls." *Esquire* 68 (1967): 59+.
———. "Stalking the Billion-Footed Beast: A Literary Manifesto for the New Social Novel." *Harper's,* Nov. 1989, 45–56.
Woodford, Frank B., and Arthur M. Woodford. *All Our Yesterdays: A Brief History of Detroit.* Detroit: Wayne State University Press, 1969.
Zieger, Rob, and David G. Grant. "Childhood's End." *Detroit News,* 1 Jan 1989, A1+.